The Essential Vegetarian Indian Cookbook

THE ESSENTIAL
Vegetarian
Indian
COOKBOOK

125 Classic Recipes to Enjoy at Home

Pavani Nandula

Photography by Hélène Dujardin

ROCKRIDGE
PRESS

Interior and Cover Designer: Stephanie Mautone
Art Producer: Hannah Dickerson
Editor: Gurvinder Singh Gandu
Production Editor: Rachel Taenzler
Photography © 2020 Hélène Dujardin.
Food styling by Anna Hampton, assisted by Lisa Rovick.
All decorative patterns used under license from Shutterstock.com.

ISBN: Print 978-1-64739-737-1 | eBook 978-1-64739-439-4
R0

To Harsha, Dhruva, and Disha:
This would not have been possible
without your love and support.

Chole Masala page 175

Contents

Introduction

My passion for food and cooking began in my childhood. I grew up in a vegetarian family in Hyderabad, a bustling city in the state of Telangana, India. In those days, my mom, who has always been an excellent cook and my biggest culinary inspiration, always cooked lip-smackingly good meals, snacks, and desserts from scratch at home with an emphasis on plant-based food. In fact, I do not remember us ever buying snacks from the store.

Growing up, I loved watching Indian cooking shows, and my mom encouraged me to make the recipes featured on those shows. And that was how my cooking journey sort of began. But it was not until I moved to the United States in the early 2000s for graduate school that I really started cooking full-time.

As a vegetarian, my first few months in the United States were challenging. Back then, finding Indian vegetables, spices, or even rice was a little difficult. But I managed and got creative with the local veggies and ingredients that the supermarkets offered. For example, zucchini became a good replacement for Indian opo squash, and new-to-me veggies such as broccoli and asparagus were adapted to Indian dishes.

Trying out new dishes for my friends and receiving their positive feedback got me cooking even more. In 2006, I started my blog, *Cook's Hideout*, to document my everyday kitchen experiments. I love sharing my vegetarian dishes with friends from different ethnicities, and they are always pleasantly surprised by the variety that Indian cuisine has to offer.

A large proportion of the Indian population is vegetarian, mostly due to religious beliefs and economic necessities. India is a secular country with many religions that consider vegetarianism as a most important virtue. As a result, many Indians abstain from eating meats, fish, and poultry. Instead, the emphasis is placed on fresh vegetables, fruits, legumes, and dairy products. Even among the households that eat meat, vegetables and vegetarian dishes play an equal part in everyday meals. Moreover, meat is expensive in India, so budget constraints are a strong driving force behind the adoption of a vegetarian diet.

In writing this book, my goal is to encourage you to make your favorite Indian dishes at home. The book offers tons of scrumptious vegetarian recipes that are simple to make and do not need any special cooking equipment or techniques. Ingredients for these recipes are also easy to source in local grocery stores or stores that specialize in Indian ingredients. I've included fan-favorite recipes that you might have tasted at an Indian restaurant, and I've also added some recipes that you may not be familiar with, to give you plenty of variety.

Indian cuisine is arguably one of the most diverse and versatile in the world. Its use of spices and ingredients can be intimidating in the beginning. But, as you try the recipes, you will learn how different spices and herbs interact with each other as well as other ingredients to create unique flavors. Learning this will help you unlock the magic of Indian cooking. Feel free to experiment with the spices and their flavors to understand how they appeal to your taste buds.

My hope is that you dive into vegetarian Indian cooking with confidence and really enjoy making these recipes for your family and friends. Happy cooking!

1

Your Vegetarian Indian Kitchen

Indian cuisine is amazingly diverse and versatile. Each region of India has its own style, identity, and flavor profile based on the local culture and ingredient availability. Despite all these differences, there is, however, a common thread that runs through the various regions: the use of spices. Each region's cuisine draws from the huge spectrum of spices and uses them in different proportions to create distinct tastes. This section will help familiarize you with certain cooking techniques as well as the key spices and ingredients that are used throughout this book.

Keys to Mastering Indian Cooking at Home

Here are a few cooking techniques and tips that will help you get comfortable with making your favorite Indian dishes.

Bhunao (sautéing): This simple technique is used in most Indian recipes for creating rich and deeply flavorful sauces. Bhunao is the process of cooking over medium-to-high heat; adding small quantities of liquid, such as water or tomato puree; and stirring constantly to prevent the ingredients from sticking.

Tadka (tempering): Tadka is unique to Indian cooking. Whole spices are added to hot oil to extract and retain their essence, aroma, and flavor. Tempering is usually done either at the beginning of cooking or when cooking has finished.

Dum (steaming): This very traditional cooking technique is used to make casserole-type dishes. It is a slow cooking method in which food is cooked under steam to ensure that all the flavors are retained in the dish.

Roasting spices: Roasting removes the raw smell of spices and intensifies their flavor by heating the essential oils within the spice.

Buy whole spices: It is best to buy dry spices in their whole form and then grind them as necessary. They stay fresh longer in their whole state than when ground.

Plan ahead: Getting ready for a party? Plan the menu at least two to three days in advance. Pick recipes that can be made ahead of time. Most curries, dals, and desserts can be made at least two days in advance. Plan to make only one or two dishes on the day of the party. Make sure to read through the recipes completely at least twice to make sure you have the ingredients and instructions clear.

Mise en place: This French culinary term, which means "put in place," works for Indian cooking as well. Measuring all the ingredients, especially spices and produce, and getting them prepped before starting will make the cooking process that much easier.

Use fresh herbs: Always use fresh herbs, such as fresh cilantro and mint, for the best flavor.

Kitchen Equipment

Cooking authentic Indian food at home does not require any special tools or equipment. You likely already have what you need in your kitchen. That said, there are a few tools that, while not absolutely essential, I find handy to make cooking simpler and more efficient.

Blender: Super useful for making spice blends, chutneys, and purees. I have a small spice grinder to make freshly ground spice powders and pastes. I also have a slightly more powerful blender to make dosa batters and smooth gravies for curries. You could use an immersion blender instead, which comes in handy when blending hot liquids right in the pan.

Cookware: I prefer sturdy nonstick and stainless-steel cookware because Indian cooking generally involves long cooking times, and thin pans might burn the bottom of the food.

Kadai: This small, round-bottomed wok is used to deep-fry foods. The round bottom creates a deeper frying surface area that requires less oil than a flat-bottomed pot with straight edges. A small wok could work as well.

Mortar and pestle: This traditional tool is used to crush and grind spices. I use a mortar and pestle to grind spices in smaller quantities; otherwise I prefer a spice grinder or a food processor for speed and efficiency.

Pressure cooker: This is a quintessential appliance in Indian kitchens. It cooks dried legumes in less water, faster, and with greater retention of vitamins and minerals than traditional cooking methods. I have quite a few pressure cookers in different sizes for different uses: one to make lentils, one for rice, etc. Recently, Instant Pots have taken the place of pressure cookers in my kitchen. They are fuss-free and nearly hands-free.

Tawa (griddle): A large, round, cast-iron or stainless-steel skillet or griddle is perfect for making dosa or Indian flatbreads such as roti or paratha.

Spices and Other Pantry Staples

Indian cooking is all about spices. You may not be familiar with some of the spices you'll come across in this book, but don't worry; you'll soon get used to them. I've listed several here so you can begin to get acquainted. Chapter 9 has recipes for widely used spice blends, such as Garam Masala (page 164) and Tandoori Masala (page 165) that are used in many of the recipes in this book.

Spices

Asafetida (hing): This is a dried resin from a fennel-like plant that has a strong pungent flavor. A little goes a long way with this spice. Buy the ground version instead of the block for ease of use and because it tastes mellower.

Bay leaves: Dried bay leaves are commonly used in Indian cooking. They can be used whole to flavor curries and rice dishes, or they can be dry roasted and ground to make spice blends.

Black salt (kala namak): This type of salt has a strong sulfuric odor but a pleasant smoky taste. It is used in Chaat Masala (page 166) to give the spice blend its characteristic flavor.

Cardamom (elaichi): There are two types of cardamom used in Indian cooking: small green pods and large black pods. The green pods are very aromatic and are commonly used in many Indian dishes, especially desserts. Black pods are slightly bitter and are used mostly in North Indian dishes.

Chaat masala: This spice blend is used as seasoning for snacks known as chaat (meaning "to lick" in Hindi). It is flavorful and adds a punch to dishes.

Cumin seed (jeera): This is one of the most widely used spices in Indian cooking. It is either used whole or in powder form (roasted and ground). Cumin has a warm, nutty flavor that enhances any dish.

Dry mango powder (amchur powder): Tart green mango slices are sun-dried and ground to a powder. This adds a tart, sour flavor to North Indian dishes particularly stir-frys and dry curries.

Garam masala: This is arguably the most popular Indian spice blend, adding flavor to any dish. It is available in most grocery stores or you can make your own (page 164).

Mustard seeds: These tiny round seeds have a hot, pungent flavor. They are available as yellow, brown, or black seeds. Black seeds (called "rai") are used in Indian cooking, either whole or powdered.

Turmeric: Fresh turmeric is a rhizome, like gingerroot. Ground turmeric has a vibrant color and a bitter taste that mellows after cooking. This is another spice where a little goes a long way.

Lentils and Legumes

Dried legumes and lentils are an integral part of Indian cuisine because they are economical and are a wonderfully nutritious source of protein, fiber, minerals, and vitamins. Broadly known as "dal," virtually every traditional Indian meal incorporates lentils in one form of another.

Here are the lentils and legumes that are used in this book's recipes:

Black-eyed peas (lobhia): These have a buttery, creamy taste and are easy to cook from their dry state. Canned and frozen black-eyed peas are widely available in grocery stores.

Black lentils (urad dal): Black lentils come in four different forms: whole, whole skinned, split, and split skinned. Look for these in the Indian food section of your grocery store, or pay a visit to a store that specializes in Indian ingredients.

Chickpeas (kabuli chana): Chickpeas are one of the most popular and versatile legumes. They have a nutty texture and can easily absorb spices and flavors, making them perfect to use in spicy Indian curries such as Chana Masala (page 82). Canned chickpeas are the most convenient pantry staple to stock up on.

Mung beans (moong dal): The most common forms of mung beans are whole and split skinned varieties. Mung beans cook really fast in both whole and split forms. They are widely available in grocery stores.

Pigeon peas (toor dal): This pea variety is available in both whole and split versions. All of the recipes in this book use the split skinned version because they are both easy to find and faster to cook. Pigeon peas form the base for many dal recipes, such as Sambar (page 87) and Dal Tadka (page 84).

Red kidney beans (rajma): These beans are very popular in North India, especially in Punjab. They have a hearty texture and aroma that work well in Rajma Masala (page 83) and Dal Makhani (page 80).

Red lentils (masoor dal): Popular all over the world and mostly used in their split skinned form, red lentils cook quickly and have a very smooth texture, making them perfect for soups and dals.

Yellow split peas (chana dal): These peas are split and hulled. They are quite firm and tend to keep their shape even after cooking for a long time. Their nutty flavor and texture make Dal Tadka (page 84) and Panchmel Dal (page 91) crowd favorites.

Grains and Flour

Rice and/or roti (Indian flatbreads) are an integral part of every meal in India. They act as a vehicle for curries and many other types of dishes.

Rice: There are many varieties of rice grown and sold on the Indian subcontinent. The type of rice used in everyday cooking varies from region to region. South Indians prefer locally available medium- to long-grain rice, such as the sona masoori variety. Northerners prefer the more aromatic long-grain basmati rice, which grows in the foothills of the Himalayas. Basmati is the most popular and the most expensive rice. It has a wonderful fragrance, it absorbs flavors beautifully, and it also keeps its shape during cooking.

Brown basmati is also widely available. These grains still have the bran layer intact, making them rich in fiber, protein, vitamins, and minerals. Brown rice may be substituted for white rice, but brown rice requires more water to cook and takes longer. Soaking the rice ahead of time tenderizes the grain and makes for faster and more even cooking.

SOAK AND COOK TIMES

Soaking legumes, especially whole beans, helps them cook faster. It also makes them more easily digestible. Cooking times vary based on the type of legume and the cooking method. Cooking legumes the old-fashioned way on the stovetop takes longer, whereas pressure cooking expedites the process, especially for dried legumes such as kidney beans, chickpeas, etc. Please note that all pressure cookers work slightly differently, so there could be some variation in the following cooking times.

LEGUME/LENTIL	SOAKING TIME	COOKING TIME	
		STOVETOP	PRESSURE COOK
Basmati rice	30 minutes	15 to 20 minutes	5 to 7 minutes
Black-eyed peas	4 to 6 hours	45 minutes	8 to 10 minutes
Black lentils	8 to 10 hours	1 hour	12 to 15 minutes
Brown basmati rice	1 to 2 hours	40 to 45 minutes	18 to 20 minutes
Chickpeas	8 to 10 hours	1 to 2 hours	10 to 14 minutes
Mung beans, split	-	20 minutes	5 to 6 minutes
Mung beans, whole	1 hour	30 minutes	8 minutes
Pigeon peas, split	-	40 minutes	8 minutes
Red kidney beans	8 to 10 hours	1 hour	12 to 14 minutes
Red lentils, split	-	20 minutes	5 to 6 minutes
Yellow split peas	30 minutes	45 minutes	8 to 10 minutes

Atta/chapati flour: This whole-wheat flour is used to make Indian flatbreads and is sold in stores specializing in Indian, Pakistani, and other Asian foods. Indian wheat is lower in protein than US wheat and is ideal for making fluffy, thin roti. If you do not have access to atta, then use half US whole-wheat flour and half all-purpose flour in recipes calling for atta.

Chickpea flour (besan): Made from dried chickpeas, this pale-yellow flour is high in dietary fiber and protein. It is used to make Vegetable Pakoras (page 14) and soft Missi Roti (page 111).

Fresh and Refrigerated Items

Many of the savory dishes in this book call for some basic fresh and refrigerated ingredients that are readily available in most grocery stores.

Chile peppers: Fresh chiles are very important in Indian cooking for adding heat and pungency to dishes. Generally, smaller chiles are hotter than larger ones. I use fresh Thai and serrano chiles in my everyday cooking. I remove the membrane and seeds to tone down the heat. Dried red chiles such as cayenne or chile de arbol are also widely used in Indian cooking.

Cilantro (coriander leaves): These are used both as a garnish and as an ingredient. I store fresh cilantro in the refrigerator wrapped in paper towels in a resealable plastic bag. It stays fresh for four to five days.

Fenugreek (methi leaves): Fresh methi is sold in bunches in most Indian and Asian grocery stores along with cilantro and mint. These leaves have a slightly bitter flavor that goes well in curries. The dried version is called kasoori methi and is used in curry sauces to add a unique flavor and aroma.

Garlic (lasoon): Garlic is used extensively in Indian cooking to add assertive flavor. It is also widely used in combination with ginger in many curries and rice dishes. You can find a recipe for Ginger-Garlic Paste on page 172.

Ghee: This is one of the primary cooking fats in India. Ghee is available in many regular grocery stores, but making it at home is very easy. A recipe for homemade ghee can be found on page 167.

Ginger (adrak): Fresh ginger is a very common ingredient throughout India. It is often ground into paste or finely grated. Look for a fresh, heavy root that snaps easily. Store in the refrigerator for up to 3 weeks or in the freezer for extended storage.

Mint leaves: Fresh mint is used in marinades, chutneys, rice dishes, and curries. The spearmint variety is more common in Indian cooking. When buying mint, make sure the leaves are fresh and green without any brown or black spots. I store mint like cilantro, in the refrigerator.

Tamarind: This is a pod of the tamarind tree. It has a sour and slightly sweet taste that helps balance the spiciness of some Indian dishes. Tamarind is sold in various forms: in blocks, pods, and in jars of paste or concentrate. All the recipes in this book call for tamarind concentrate because it is the most convenient form to use.

Tomatoes: These form the basis of many sauces and gravies in Indian cuisine. I use tomatoes on the vine or the Roma variety for their juiciness and slight sourness that goes well with spices. I also keep canned diced tomatoes on hand in case I run out of fresh.

Yogurt: Yogurt is made fresh almost every day in households around India. It is served with almost every meal either as a raita (salad) or just plain. Store-bought whole-milk plain yogurt is the best to use for consistency and flavor. Homemade yogurt is simple to make, and you can find a recipe on page 168.

About the Recipes

If you know your way around an Indian menu, you may already be familiar with many of the recipes in this book. I've included some of those fan favorites that you might have enjoyed at Indian restaurants. There are also some less familiar dishes to give you variety. The recipes are divided into chapters that correlate to the components of a meal, so you'll find everything you need to make an authentic and wonderfully aromatic and delicious Indian meal. The final chapter contains recipes for some commonly used staples in Indian cooking. To help you create a meal plan for everyday dining or for entertaining, I have included a few menu ideas (page 179) to get you started.

You'll see that many recipes have tips; these provide suggestions for the preparation of an ingredient, a substitute ingredient in case of a food allergy or you don't have an ingredient on hand, or an idea for tweaking the recipe.

Tikki Chaat page 15

2
Appetizers and Snacks

Spinach and Paneer Samosas

PREP TIME: 40 minutes   COOK TIME: 20 minutes   TOTAL TIME: 1 hour

Samosas are crispy, deep-fried stuffed pastries and are the most popular savory snack in India. Traditionally, they are filled with spicy mashed potatoes and peas, but my version includes grated paneer and spinach to add extra color and flavor. Samosas are usually served with Cilantro Mint Chutney (page 134) and Tamarind Chutney (page 135). SERVES 6

1½ cups all-purpose flour

1¼ teaspoons salt, divided

¼ cup vegetable or canola oil, divided, plus more for deep-frying

¼ cup water

½ teaspoon cumin seeds

2 green chile peppers, finely chopped

1 medium onion, finely chopped

2 medium russet potatoes, boiled, peeled, and mashed

1 cup grated paneer, store-bought or homemade (page 170)

3 cups spinach leaves, coarsely chopped

¼ teaspoon ground turmeric

½ teaspoon Garam Masala (page 164)

3 tablespoons finely chopped fresh cilantro

1. In a medium mixing bowl, whisk together the flour and ½ teaspoon of salt. Add 3 tablespoons of oil and rub it in with your fingers until the mixture resembles coarse sand. Slowly add the water and mix until a stiff dough forms, adding more water if needed.

2. Knead the dough until it's smooth and pliable, 4 to 6 minutes. Place the dough in a lightly greased bowl, cover, and set aside for 30 minutes.

3. While the dough rests, heat 1 tablespoon of oil in a medium skillet over medium heat. Add the cumin seeds and, once they start to sizzle, add the chiles and onion. Cook for 3 to 4 minutes or until the onions are lightly browned around the edges.

4. Stir in the potatoes, paneer, spinach, turmeric, garam masala, and the remaining ¾ teaspoon of salt. Mix well to combine. Cook for 4 to 5 minutes. Turn off the heat and stir in the cilantro. Set aside to cool.

5. Divide the pastry into 6 equal pieces. Work with one dough piece at a time and keep the rest covered with a kitchen towel to avoid drying out.

6. Roll out the ball into a 6-inch round, then cut it in half. Take one half-circle and form a cone by folding the dough in half and sealing the cut edges together. Wet the edges with a little water before sealing to ensure that the dough sticks to itself.

7. Fill the cone with 2 tablespoons of filling. Make sure not to overfill, to avoid the filling oozing out when frying. Close the top edge firmly by pressing the dough together. Use a fork to pinch it closed. Repeat with the remaining pieces of dough.

8. Fill a medium wok or heavy-bottomed skillet 2 inches deep with oil and heat over medium-high heat to 350°F. Working in batches, carefully slide the filled samosas into the hot oil and fry until golden-brown and crispy.

9. Using a slotted spoon, transfer the fried samosas to a paper towel–lined plate. Serve hot or at room temperature.

Tip: To save time, use store-bought pie dough or puff pastry. Fill the pastries according to the recipe, but instead of frying, bake these samosas in a 375°F oven for 30 minutes.

Vegetable Pakora

PREP TIME: 20 minutes   **COOK TIME:** 20 minutes   **TOTAL TIME:** 40 minutes

These fried fritters, known as bhajiyas or bajji, are a popular teatime snack all over India. This savory snack can be made in many ways with a variety of fillings. I have used a mix of vegetables in this recipe, but you can make them with just one or two veggies. They are served hot with ketchup or with Cilantro Mint Chutney (page 134). SERVES 4

1½ cups chickpea flour (besan)

¼ teaspoon ground coriander

½ teaspoon cayenne pepper

¾ teaspoon salt

⅛ teaspoon baking soda

1 medium onion, thinly sliced

1 medium carrot, peeled and cut into thin strips

4 cups spinach leaves, coarsely chopped

1 small green bell pepper, chopped

¾ to 1 cup water

Vegetable or canola oil, for deep-frying

Chaat Masala (page 166), for sprinkling

1. In a medium mixing bowl, sift the chickpea flour to remove any lumps. Add the coriander, cayenne, salt, and baking soda, and mix well to combine.

2. Add the onion, carrot, spinach, and bell pepper to the mixing bowl and toss to coat evenly with the chickpea flour mixture. Gradually add water to make a thick batter. The spinach and onion will release water, so adjust the amount of water based on the consistency.

3. Fill a medium wok or heavy-bottomed skillet 2 inches deep with oil and heat over medium-high heat to 350°F. Working in batches, scoop a tablespoon of batter and carefully drop it into the hot oil. Fry until the pakora are evenly golden brown, turning once or twice. This will take 3 to 4 minutes.

4. Use a slotted spoon to transfer the pakora to a paper towel–lined plate. Sprinkle the pakora with chaat masala while they are still hot. Serve immediately.

Tip: To make crunchy and perfect pakora, make sure not to overcrowd the pan. Fry the batter in batches.

Tikki Chaat

PREP TIME: 30 minutes   **COOK TIME:** 45 minutes   **TOTAL TIME:** 1 hour 15 minutes

Tikki chaat is potato patties topped with chickpea sauce and mint and tamarind chutneys. It is a lip-smacking dish that is hot, spicy, tangy, and sweet all at the same time. All the components can be made ahead of time and refrigerated until you are ready. All you need to do is warm them up and serve. **SERVES 4**

1½ tablespoons vegetable
or canola oil, divided,
plus more for frying

1 small onion,
finely chopped

4 green chile peppers,
finely chopped, divided

1 ripe tomato, chopped

½ teaspoon ground cumin

½ teaspoon ground
coriander

½ teaspoon
cayenne pepper

½ teaspoon dried mango
powder (amchur)

½ teaspoon Chole Masala
(page 175)

1 (15.5-ounce) can
chickpeas, rinsed
and drained

½ cup water

1½ teaspoons salt, divided

½ teaspoon freshly ground
black pepper

3 medium russet
potatoes, boiled, peeled,
and mashed

½ cup green peas (thawed,
if using frozen)

1. Heat 1 tablespoon of oil in a medium skillet over medium heat. Add the onion and half of the chile peppers and cook for 3 to 4 minutes or until the onion turns translucent.

2. Add the tomato, cumin, coriander, cayenne, mango powder, and chole masala and cook for 2 to 3 minutes or until the tomato turns mushy.

3. Add the chickpeas, water, 1 teaspoon of salt, and the pepper. Simmer the mixture for 4 to 5 minutes. Using a potato masher, coarsely mash the chickpeas, leaving a few whole.

4. In a medium bowl, combine the potatoes, peas, cilantro, cornstarch, and the remaining ½ teaspoon of salt. Mix well.

5. Heat ½ tablespoon of oil in a small skillet over medium heat. Add the onion seeds and cumin seeds and cook for 30 seconds. Add the remaining half of the chile peppers and cook for another 30 seconds. Add this to the potato mixture and mix well to combine.

6. Divide the potato mixture into 8 equal portions. Shape and flatten them into round patties ½-inch thick.

CONTINUED ····▸

2 tablespoons finely chopped fresh cilantro

1 tablespoon cornstarch

1 teaspoon onion seeds (nigella seeds)

½ teaspoon cumin seeds

Sev (fried chickpea noodles), for serving

Tamarind Chutney (page 135), for serving

Cilantro Mint Chutney (page 134), for serving

Yogurt (page 168), whisked, for serving

Red onion, finely chopped, for serving

7. Heat a medium griddle over medium heat. Pour 2 teaspoons of oil onto the griddle and cook the patties until lightly browned on both sides, 2 to 3 minutes per side, working in batches.

8. Transfer the cooked patties to a plate and repeat with the remaining patties, adding more oil as needed.

9. To serve, place 2 potato patties in each serving bowl and top them with chickpea sauce, sev, tamarind chutney, cilantro mint chutney, a drizzle of yogurt, and a sprinkle of red onion. Serve immediately.

Tip: The chickpea sauce and potato patties can be made at least 2 days in advance. Make the patties following steps 4 through 6, cool the patties completely, and refrigerate them in an airtight container. On the day of serving, cook the patties on the griddle and serve them with the warmed sauce and other toppings.

Pav Bhaji

PREP TIME: 20 minutes **COOK TIME:** 1 hour **Total time:** 1 hour 20 minutes

Pav bhaji is one of the most beloved street foods in India. Its popularity started on the streets of Mumbai, but nowadays pav bhaji is a standard offering in many high-end restaurants as well. It is a vegetarian Indian version of Western sloppy joes. "Pav" is the bread or bun that is served with the vegetable curry, or bhaji. The key is in getting all the flavors right, so make sure to taste the seasonings as you cook. SERVES 6

2 medium potatoes, peeled and diced

2 cups cauliflower florets

½ cup green peas (no need to thaw if frozen)

4 cups water

1 tablespoon vegetable or canola oil

4 tablespoons butter, divided, plus more for the buns

1 medium green bell pepper, finely chopped

1 teaspoon Ginger-Garlic Paste (page 172)

¼ teaspoon ground turmeric

2 medium tomatoes, chopped

2 teaspoons Pav Bhaji Masala (page 174)

½ teaspoon cayenne pepper

¾ teaspoon salt

1. In a medium saucepan over medium-high heat, combine the potatoes, cauliflower, peas, and water. Bring to a boil. Lower the heat, cover the pan, and simmer until the veggies are very tender, 15 to 20 minutes.

2. Heat the oil and 1 tablespoon of butter in a large skillet or wok over medium heat. Add the bell pepper and cook until tender, 4 minutes. Stir in the ginger-garlic paste and turmeric and cook for 1 minute, stirring frequently.

3. Add the tomatoes and cook until they turn mushy, 4 minutes. Stir in the pav bhaji masala, cayenne, and salt. Cook for 1 to 2 minutes.

4. Meanwhile, drain the veggies and reserve the cooking water. Return the vegetables to the pan and mash them to a coarse paste.

CONTINUED ····▸

1 tablespoon freshly squeezed lime or lemon juice

2 tablespoons finely chopped fresh cilantro

12 slider buns or 6 burger buns, halved

1 small onion, finely chopped (optional)

1 lime, cut into wedges (optional)

5. Add the vegetable mash to the skillet along with the reserved cooking water. Mix well and cook, covered, on medium-low heat, stirring occasionally, for 12 to 15 minutes. If the bhaji looks too thick, add more water. Stir in 1 tablespoon of butter and let it melt into the bhaji. Repeat with the remaining 2 tablespoons of butter. Squeeze in the lime juice and stir well. Check the seasoning and adjust with more pav bhaji masala, salt, or cayenne, if desired.

6. Sprinkle the bhaji with the cilantro and keep it warm while you toast the buns.

7. Heat a griddle or skillet over medium heat. Butter the cut side of the buns and place them cut-side down on the hot griddle. Toast until the bottom is nicely browned, about 1 minute, then transfer to a plate.

8. To serve, place the pav (buns) and bhaji on the serving plate. Top the bhaji with onions and a squeeze of lime juice (if using).

Tip: Bhaji can be made up to 2 days in advance. Keep it refrigerated and warm it before serving. Leftover bhaji can be frozen in an airtight container for up to 2 months.

Gobi Manchurian

PREP TIME: 20 minutes   COOK TIME: 30 minutes   TOTAL TIME: 50 minutes

Gobi Manchurian is an Indian adaptation of Chinese cooking and season-ings. Gobi is Hindi for "cauliflower," so as you might expect, this recipe contains that vegetable in the form of crisp-fried fritters tossed in a spicy, tangy sauce. This dish makes a great appetizer or can be served as a side dish with Vegetable Fried Rice (page 127). SERVES 4

5 tablespoons cornstarch, divided

1 cup water, divided, plus more if needed

1 tablespoon vegetable or canola oil, plus more for deep-frying

2 teaspoons peeled grated fresh ginger

2 garlic cloves, finely minced

4 scallions, chopped

1 small green bell pepper, finely chopped

1½ tablespoons soy sauce, divided

2 teaspoons chili sauce or sriracha sauce (store-bought)

1 tablespoon tomato ketchup or tomato paste

1½ teaspoons salt, divided

1 teaspoon freshly ground black pepper, divided

1 small head cauliflower, cut into florets (3 cups)

½ cup all-purpose flour

1. In a small bowl, whisk 1 tablespoon of corn-starch with ¼ cup of water. Set aside.

2. Heat the oil in a wok or large skillet over medium-high heat. Add the ginger and garlic and cook for 30 seconds or until fragrant. Add the scallions and bell pepper and cook for 2 to 3 minutes or until crisp-tender.

3. Stir in 1 tablespoon of soy sauce, the chili sauce, ketchup, 1 teaspoon of salt, and ½ teaspoon of pepper. Cook for 30 seconds.

4. Stir in the cornstarch mixture and cook until the mixture thickens, 2 to 3 minutes. If the mix-ture looks too thick, add 1 to 2 tablespoons of water. Set aside.

5. Fill a medium saucepan with water and bring to a boil over medium-high heat. Lower the heat to medium and add the cauliflower. Simmer for 5 minutes or until the cauliflower is fork-tender. Drain completely and place on a kitchen towel to dry.

CONTINUED ····▶

6. In a mixing bowl, combine the flour, the remaining 4 tablespoons cornstarch, the remaining ½ tablespoon of soy sauce, the remaining ½ teaspoon of salt, and the remaining ½ teaspoon of pepper. Add the remaining ¾ cup of water and whisk to make a thick, pourable batter.

7. Fill a medium wok or heavy-bottomed skillet 2 inches deep with oil and heat over medium-high heat to 350°F.

8. Dip the cauliflower florets one at a time in the batter and gently add them to the hot oil. Fry in batches until lightly golden on all sides. Use a slotted spoon to transfer them to a paper towel–lined plate.

9. To serve, add the fritters to the sauce and bring to a simmer. Mix well to evenly coat the fritters with the sauce. Serve hot.

Tips: Frozen cauliflower florets can be used instead of fresh. Thaw them according to the package directions, dry the florets on a kitchen towel, and proceed with the recipe, skipping step 5.

Masala Papad

PREP TIME: 10 minutes   COOK TIME: 5 minutes   TOTAL TIME: 15 minutes

Papad, or pappadums, are crispy wafer-thin crackers that are traditionally served with chutneys at Indian restaurants. They are made with lentil flours and are usually flavored with black pepper, cumin, garlic, chili powder, etc. This recipe, which includes toppings, is a quick and easy appetizer and is sure to please your guests. Make sure to top the papad just before serving; otherwise, they will turn soggy. SERVES 4

4 papad

1 cup corn kernels (thawed, if frozen)

1 medium tomato, finely chopped

1 green chile pepper, finely chopped

2 scallions, finely chopped

½ teaspoon Chaat Masala (page 166)

½ teaspoon salt

¼ teaspoon freshly ground black pepper

1 tablespoon freshly squeezed lemon juice

1. The papad can be prepared either by heating them directly over a gas flame or by frying them in oil. They will turn crisp and brittle as they cool. Set the papad aside while you make the toppings.

2. In a small mixing bowl, combine the corn, tomato, chile, scallions, chaat masala, salt, pepper, and lemon juice. Toss well to combine. Taste and adjust the seasoning.

3. Just before serving, spread the topping evenly on the crisp papad and serve right away.

Chile Cheese Toast

PREP TIME: 10 minutes   **COOK TIME:** 10 minutes   **TOTAL TIME:** 20 minutes

Chile cheese toast is a spicy Indian take on a grilled cheese sandwich. It is served open-faced and can be as spicy as you want. Add finely chopped chiles for a nice kick. Processed cheese is commonly used in India to make this dish, but cheddar or mozzarella are excellent substitutes. Or you can use your favorite melting cheese. SERVES 4

1 cup grated cheddar or mozzarella cheese

2 scallions, finely chopped

1 small green or red chile pepper, seeded and finely chopped

1 garlic clove, minced

¼ teaspoon salt

⅛ teaspoon freshly ground black pepper

¼ teaspoon red pepper flakes

4 wholegrain or white bread slices

2 tablespoons butter, at room temperature

1. Preheat the oven to 400°F. Line a baking sheet with parchment paper.

2. In a small mixing bowl, combine the cheese, scallions, chile pepper, garlic, salt, black pepper, and red pepper flakes. Mix well to combine.

3. Butter the bread slices and place them butter-side up on the prepared baking sheet.

4. Divide the cheese mixture equally on the tops of the bread slices. Bake for 6 to 8 minutes or until the cheese has melted and the bread is well toasted. Remove from the oven and serve immediately.

Tip: Chile cheese toast can be made on the stovetop in a skillet. Place the bread slices butter-side down in the pan and cook, covered, until the cheese melts and the bread is toasted.

Okra Fries

PREP TIME: 10 minutes COOK TIME: 20 minutes TOTAL TIME: 30 minutes

Okra fries are the Indian version of Japanese tempura. These deep-fried battered okra fries are so crispy and addictive that even okra naysayers cannot get enough of them. Taming the sliminess of okra is the key to success in this recipe. Wash the okra pods in a colander and drain them very well, then lay them out on a kitchen towel for at least 30 minutes and wipe each one to remove any excess moisture. SERVES 4

½ **pound fresh okra, washed and dried (see headnote)**

½ **cup chickpea flour (besan)**

2 tablespoons cornstarch

½ **teaspoon Ginger-Garlic Paste** (page 172)

¼ **teaspoon cayenne pepper**

½ **teaspoon salt**

¼ **teaspoon turmeric**

Vegetable or canola oil, for deep-frying

2 tablespoons warm water

Coarse salt, for serving

Chaat Masala (page 166), **for serving**

1. Cut off and discard the crown end of each okra. Cut each okra pod into quarters lengthwise. (If the pod is small, just cut it in half.) Place the cut okra in a medium bowl.

2. Add the chickpea flour, cornstarch, ginger-garlic paste, cayenne, salt, and turmeric. Gently toss to combine.

3. Fill a medium wok or heavy-bottomed skillet 2 inches deep with oil and heat it over medium-high heat to 350°F.

4. Once the oil is hot, add the water to the okra mixture and mix to evenly coat the okra with the batter. Using your hands works best here.

5. Working in batches, carefully drop handfuls of battered okra into the hot oil and use a slotted spoon to separate the pieces. It is okay if they clump a little.

6. Fry until golden brown and crispy all over, 5 to 7 minutes. Use a slotted spoon to transfer the okra to a paper towel–lined plate. Sprinkle with salt and chaat masala. Serve immediately.

Tip: Make sure the chopping board and knife you use are completely dry. Any moisture on these will also make the okra slimy.

Vada Pav

PREP TIME: 20 minutes   COOK TIME: 20 minutes   TOTAL TIME: 40 minutes

Vada pav, an Indian-style burger, is a popular street food in Mumbai. Vada, the burger, is made with spicy potato fried in a chickpea batter. Pav is the bun. Cilantro Mint Chutney (page 134) is smeared on the bread and gives this sandwich an amazing flavor. This is a scrumptious and filling snack that can be eaten as a mini-meal. SERVES 6

2 teaspoons vegetable or canola oil, plus more for deep-frying

½ teaspoon mustard seeds

1 teaspoon Ginger-Garlic Paste (page 172)

2 large russet potatoes, peeled, boiled, and mashed

½ teaspoon ground coriander

1 teaspoon cayenne pepper, divided

½ teaspoon dried mango powder (amchur)

1½ teaspoons salt, divided

1 tablespoon finely chopped fresh cilantro

¾ cup chickpea flour (besan)

¼ cup rice flour

⅛ teaspoon baking soda

¼ cup water

6 slider buns or Hawaiian rolls

Cilantro Mint Chutney (page 134), **for serving**

1. Heat the oil in a medium pan over medium heat. Add the mustard seeds. Once they start to pop, add the ginger-garlic paste. Cook for 30 seconds or until fragrant.

2. Add the potatoes, coriander, ½ teaspoon cayenne pepper, amchur, and 1 teaspoon of salt. Mix well to combine and cook for 3 to 4 minutes to heat through. Stir in the cilantro. Set aside to cool.

3. Once it is cool enough to handle, divide the mixture into 8 equal parts and shape them into rounds.

4. Combine the chickpea flour, rice flour, the remaining ½ teaspoon of cayenne, cumin, the remaining ½ teaspoon of salt, and baking soda in a medium bowl. Whisk in the water gradually to form a thick batter with no lumps. The batter should coat the back of a spoon.

5. Fill a medium wok or heavy-bottomed skillet 2 inches deep with oil and heat it over medium-high heat to 350°F.

6. Once the oil is hot, dip a potato round into the batter to coat it. Carefully slide it into the hot oil. Repeat with 3 or 4 more rounds depending on the size of the pan. Make sure not to overcrowd the pan. Fry until the vada are golden on all sides, 4 to 5 minutes. Use a slotted spoon to transfer the vada to a paper towel–lined plate. Repeat with the remaining potato rounds.

7. Slice the buns in half and spread some chutney on the bottom bun. Place a vada on top. Spread more chutney on the top bun and place it over the vada. Flatten it slightly and enjoy.

Bhel Puri

PREP TIME: 15 minutes

Bhel puri is a quick and easy dish to make and provides tangy, spicy, and sweet flavors. Traditional bhel puri is made with just potato, but this version includes other veggies as well. SERVES 6

1 small **potato, peeled, cubed, and boiled**

2 medium **tomatoes, seeded and finely chopped**

1 small **cucumber, seeded and finely chopped**

1 small **red onion, finely chopped**

¼ cup **frozen green peas, thawed**

¼ cup **frozen corn kernels, thawed**

1 small **carrot, peeled and grated**

2 **green chile peppers, finely chopped**

1 teaspoon **Chaat Masala** (page 166)

2 tablespoons **roasted peanuts**

½ teaspoon **salt** (optional)

2 cups **puffed rice**

1 tablespoon **Tamarind Chutney** (page 135)

1 tablespoon **Cilantro Mint Chutney** (page 134)

3 tablespoons **finely chopped fresh cilantro**

1 tablespoon **freshly squeezed lemon juice**

1 cup **sev (fried chickpea noodles)** (optional)

1 cup **crushed papdi (crisp flatbread)** (optional)

1. In a large mixing bowl, combine the potato, tomatoes, cucumber, onion, peas, corn, carrot, and peppers. Add the chaat masala, peanuts, and salt (if using), and toss well to combine. Set aside.

2. When ready to serve, add the puffed rice, tamarind and mint chutneys, cilantro, and lemon juice. Mix well to coat all the ingredients evenly with the chutneys. Taste and adjust the seasonings. Top with the sev and papdi. Serve immediately.

Tips: Combine the veggies and refrigerate them until ready to use. Add all the other ingredients just before serving. Indian grocery stores sell "bhel" mix, which is essentially a mixture of puffed rice, sev, and papdi. Toss this with the veggies and sauces to make instant bhel.

You can prepare the chutneys up to three days in advance, but this colorful Indian salad is best served immediately after making it.

Aloo Vegetable Bonda

PREP TIME: 15 minutes   **COOK TIME:** 30 minutes   **TOTAL TIME:** 45 minutes

I have so many fond memories of these deliciously addictive vegetable-filled fritters. They were made almost every time we visited our maternal uncles' home, and we kids used to help make the vegetable balls, having a grand time chitchatting and being the taste testers. Mashed potatoes act as a binder for all the colorful veggies that go into the filling. The veggie rounds are dipped in a spiced chickpea batter and fried until crispy and golden. They're perfect served hot with Masala Chai (page 148). **SERVES 6**

1 cup chickpea flour (besan)

¼ cup rice flour

1 teaspoon cayenne pepper, divided

¼ teaspoon ground cumin

1½ teaspoons salt, divided

⅛ teaspoon baking soda

¼ to ⅓ cup water

2 teaspoons vegetable or canola oil, plus more for deep-frying

½ teaspoon mustard seeds

1 small carrot, peeled and finely chopped

¼ cup corn kernels (thawed if frozen)

¼ cup green peas (thawed if frozen)

2 medium russet potatoes, peeled, boiled, and mashed

¼ teaspoon ground turmeric

1. Sift the chickpea flour and rice flour into a medium bowl. Add ½ teaspoon of cayenne, the cumin, ½ teaspoon of salt, and the baking soda. Whisk in ¼ cup of water, adding more if needed, until a thick, pourable batter forms that coats the back of a spoon. Set aside.

2. Heat the oil in a medium skillet over medium heat. Add the mustard seeds, and once they start to splutter, add the carrot and cook until tender, 3 to 4 minutes. Stir in the corn, peas, and potatoes, and mix well until combined.

3. Stir in the turmeric, remaining ½ teaspoon of cayenne, garam masala, mango powder, and the remaining 1 teaspoon of salt. Taste and adjust the seasonings. Let the filling cool, then divide the mixture into 12 to 15 equal-size balls.

4. Fill a medium wok or heavy-bottomed skillet 2 inches deep with oil and heat it over medium-high heat to 350°F.

CONTINUED ····▸

½ **teaspoon Garam Masala** (page 164)

½ **teaspoon dried mango powder (amchur)**

Tomato ketchup, for serving

Cilantro Mint Chutney, for serving (page 134)

5. Once the oil is ready, dip a vegetable ball into the batter to coat it evenly. Carefully slide it into the hot oil. Repeat with 3 or 4 more balls, depending on the size of the pan; make sure not to over-crowd it. Fry until the vada are golden on all sides, 4 to 5 minutes. Use a slotted spoon to transfer them to a paper towel–lined plate. Repeat with the remaining potato balls.

6. Serve hot or warm with ketchup or Cilantro Mint Chutney.

Onion Kachori

PREP TIME: 20 minutes, plus 30 minutes to rest
COOK TIME: 40 minutes   **TOTAL TIME:** 1 hour, 30 minutes

Kachori is served either as a snack or breakfast in parts of north central and northwestern India. These little crispy fried breads are often eaten with a spicy potato curry. Traditionally, spicy lentils are used as filling, but this recipe uses caramelized onions with spices. Try them! They're addictively good. **SERVES 6**

2 cups all-purpose flour

1½ teaspoons salt, divided

¼ cup **Ghee** (page 167)

½ cup water

2 teaspoons vegetable or canola oil, plus more for deep-frying

2 teaspoons onion seeds (nigella seeds)

1 bay leaf

2 green chile peppers, finely chopped

2 large onions, finely chopped

2 tablespoons chickpea flour (besan)

1 teaspoon ground coriander

1 teaspoon cayenne pepper

1 teaspoon Garam Masala (page 164)

3 tablespoons cilantro, chopped

1. In a medium bowl, whisk together the flour and ½ teaspoon salt. Add the ghee and rub with your fingers until the mixture resembles coarse sand. Slowly add the water and mix into a smooth dough. Knead for 5 to 6 minutes until the dough is soft and pliable. Cover and set aside to rest for at least 30 minutes.

2. Heat the oil in a skillet over medium heat. Add the nigella seeds, bay leaf, chiles, and onions. Sauté until the onions turn light brown, stirring occasionally.

3. Stir in the chickpea flour, coriander, cayenne, garam masala, and the remaining salt. Mix well and cook for 2 to 3 minutes. Stir in the cilantro. Remove and discard the bay leaf. Allow the mixture to cool completely.

CONTINUED ····▸

4. Divide the dough into 12 equal portions. Work with 1 dough ball at a time and keep the rest covered with a kitchen towel to prevent them from drying out. Roll out the ball into a 3-inch circle. Place 1½ teaspoons of onion filling in the center of the circle. Cover the filling by slowly stretching the dough over the filling. Seal the ends well. Using your palm, flatten the ball slightly by pressing on it. Place on a plate and keep covered while you stuff the remaining dough balls.

5. Fill a medium wok or heavy-bottomed skillet 2 inches deep with oil and heat it over medium-high heat to 350°F. Test the oil to see if the temperature is right by dropping a tiny ball of dough in the oil. If it rises slowly to the top, the oil is ready.

6. Carefully slide the kachori into the hot oil. It will drop to the bottom of the pan and rise slowly to the top. Use the back of the slotted spoon to gently keep it submerged until it puffs up. Gently flip the kachori and fry until golden on both sides. Use the slotted spoon to transfer it to a paper towel–lined plate. Repeat with the remaining kachori. Serve hot or warm.

Tip: Make sure to always keep the dough covered; if you do not, it will dry out and will not puff up.

Momos

PREP TIME: 20 minutes   COOK TIME: 20 minutes   TOTAL TIME: 40 minutes

Momos are a version of dumplings that are native to Nepal and some parts of Tibet. Because of the large Nepalese population in Sikkim, a northeastern Indian state, these are eaten in India as well. Meat- or cheese-filled momos are quite popular, but this vegan version is equally delicious. The recipe includes instructions to make the dough, but store-bought dumpling wrappers can be used instead if you're short on time. SERVES 6

1 cup all-purpose flour

1 teaspoon salt, divided

4 teaspoons vegetable or canola oil, divided

¼ to ⅓ cup water

½ cup cabbage, shredded

1 small carrot, peeled and grated

¼ cup chopped broccoli

2 or 3 medium mushrooms

1 teaspoon peeled grated fresh ginger

1 garlic clove, minced

1 green chile pepper, finely chopped

½ cup tofu, crumbled

1. Combine the flour, ½ teaspoon of salt, and 2 teaspoons of oil in a medium bowl. Slowly add the water, starting with ¼ cup and adding more if needed to form a dough. Knead into a smooth dough. Cover the bowl and set aside while you make the filling.

2. Put the cabbage, carrot, broccoli, and mushrooms in a food processor and process until finely chopped.

3. Heat the remaining 2 teaspoons of oil in a skillet over medium-high heat. Add the ginger, garlic, and chile. Cook for 30 to 45 seconds or until fragrant. Add the veggies from the food processor and cook for 6 to 8 minutes, or until they no longer smell raw. Stir in the tofu and the remaining ½ teaspoon of salt. Cook for 1 minute, then remove from the heat and set aside to cool completely.

CONTINUED ····▸

4. On a lightly oiled work surface, roll out the dough into a ¼-inch-thick circle. Use a 3-inch cookie cutter to punch out dough rounds. Working with 1 round at a time, place 2 teaspoons of filling in the center and fold the dough over to encase the filling. Pinch the edges well to seal properly. Place the filled momo on a lightly floured plate and keep it covered to prevent it from drying out. Repeat with the remaining rounds and filling.

5. Bring a steamer basket with water to a boil over high heat. Place the momos on a lightly greased plate and steam them for 6 to 8 minutes, or until they turn opaque.

6. Serve the momos hot with soy sauce or chili sauce.

Tips: Because this is a Chinese-inspired recipe, the filling uses tofu. But crumbled paneer can be used instead. Simply use ½ cup of crumbled paneer and follow the instructions in the recipe.

Dahi Vada

PREP TIME: 30 minutes, plus 4 hours to soak
COOK TIME: 30 minutes   TOTAL TIME: 5 hours

Dahi vada are creamy, spicy, fluffy lentil fritters. They are made with split skinned black lentils (urad dal) that need to be soaked for at least 4 hours, so a little bit of pre-planning is required, but the wait is well worth it. The lentil fritters are soaked in a simple yogurt sauce and topped with chutneys and are Just. So. Good! SERVES 6

1 cup split skinned black lentils

2 or 3 green chile peppers, chopped

1 teaspoon peeled grated fresh ginger

⅛ teaspoon asafetida (hing)

1 tablespoon raisins

2 tablespoons cashews, chopped

2 teaspoons salt, divided

1 cup water, divided

1 cup Yogurt (page 168), **whisked**

1 teaspoon sugar

½ teaspoon ground cumin

Vegetable or canola oil, for deep-frying

Tamarind Chutney (page 135)

Cilantro Mint Chutney (page 134)

Chaat Masala (page 166), **for sprinkling**

Cayenne pepper

2 tablespoons finely chopped fresh cilantro

1. Rinse the lentils 2 or 3 times, put them in a pot or bowl, and cover them with water. Leave the lentils to soak for at least 4 hours or overnight.

2. Drain the lentils and put them in a food processor or blender with the chile peppers, ginger, asafetida, raisins, cashews, 1 teaspoon of salt, and ¾ cup of water. Blend until the mixture is very smooth, adding more water if needed to get the desired consistency. Transfer the batter to a bowl.

3. Whisk the batter by hand vigorously for 3 to 4 minutes, to make it airy. This results in very fluffy fritters instead of dense ones.

4. In a medium bowl, combine the yogurt, sugar, the remaining 1 teaspoon of salt, and cumin, and mix well to combine. Chill until ready to use.

5. Fill a medium bowl with warm water and keep it ready.

6. Fill a medium wok or heavy-bottomed skillet 2 inches deep with oil and heat it over medium-high heat to 350°F.

CONTINUED ····▸

7. To test if the oil is hot enough, drop a tiny piece of batter into it. If the batter rises to the top, the oil is ready. Take a tablespoon of batter and use another spoon to gently slide it into the oil. Depending on the size of the pan, fry 3 or 4 fritters at a time. Fry, turning occasionally, until the fritters are golden brown and crisp on all sides. Use a slotted spoon to transfer the fritters to the warm water. Repeat with the remaining batter.

8. Working with 1 fritter at a time, press it between your palms to remove excess water. Drop it into the yogurt sauce and toss gently to coat the fritter evenly. Remove and place it on a serving platter. Repeat with the remaining fritters.

9. Pour any leftover yogurt sauce on top of the fritters. Top with chutneys and chaat masala and sprinkle with cayenne and the cilantro. Serve right away or refrigerate until ready to serve.

Paneer Tikka

PREP TIME: 10 minutes, plus 30 minutes to marinate
COOK TIME: 20 minutes   **TOTAL TIME:** 1 hour

Tikka literally means a "chunk" of meat or vegetable in Hindi. In this recipe, chunks of paneer and veggies are marinated with Tandoori Masala (page 165) and yogurt. Traditionally, tikka is cooked in a tandoor or a charcoal-fired clay oven, but a grill pan or a broiler is a good alternative. SERVES 4

½ **cup Yogurt** (page 168)

1 **tablespoon vegetable or canola oil, plus more for brushing**

1 **teaspoon Ginger-Garlic Paste** (page 172)

½ **teaspoon ground cumin**

1 **teaspoon Tandoori Masala** (page 165)

1 **teaspoon salt**

1 **tablespoon freshly squeezed lemon juice**

2 **cups paneer, store-bought or homemade** (page 170), **cut into 1-inch cubes**

1 **small green bell pepper, seeded and cut into chunks**

1 **small red or yellow bell pepper, seeded and cut into chunks**

8 **small mushrooms**

1 **large red onion, cut into chunks**

3 **tablespoons finely chopped fresh cilantro**

1. In a medium bowl, whisk together the yogurt, oil, ginger-garlic paste, cumin, tandoori masala, salt, and lemon juice. Add the paneer, bell peppers, mushrooms, and onion, and toss to coat with the marinade. Cover and set aside for at least 30 minutes.

2. Thread the paneer on metal skewers alternating with the peppers, mushrooms, and onion.

3. Heat a grill pan over medium heat and generously coat its surface with oil. Place the skewers on the grill and cook for 2 to 3 minutes, or until the paneer has nice grill marks. Repeat until all sides are grilled and the veggies are tender. Sprinkle the skewers with the cilantro and serve hot.

Tips: Bamboo skewers can be used, but make sure to first soak them in water for 20 to 30 minutes so they won't burn. For a vegan version of tikka, substitute tofu for the paneer and replace the yogurt with a nondairy yogurt (coconut or almond work great). This recipe can be made in the oven as well. Preheat the broiler on high and place the skewers on an aluminum foil–lined baking sheet. Broil for 3 to 4 minutes per side, or until the paneer and veggies are cooked and slightly charred.

Palak Paneer page 40

3
Eggs and Dairy

Anda Bhurji

PREP TIME: 5 minutes   **COOK TIME:** 10 minutes   **TOTAL TIME:** 15 minutes

This spicy Indian version of scrambled eggs is quick and easy to make for breakfast or even as part of a meal. Use any vegetables that you like or want to use up. Finely chopped bell peppers, grated carrot, and thinly sliced cabbage are all good options to add to this recipe. Serve with toasted bread for breakfast or wrap it up in Methi Roti (page 110) or Naan (page 108) for a filling meal. **SERVES 4**

2 teaspoons vegetable or canola oil

1 medium onion, finely chopped

1 teaspoon Ginger-Garlic Paste (page 172)

1 green chile pepper, finely chopped

1 medium tomato, finely chopped

¼ teaspoon Garam Masala (page 164)

½ teaspoon salt

¼ teaspoon freshly ground black pepper

4 large eggs, whisked

2 tablespoons finely chopped fresh cilantro

1. Heat the oil in a medium skillet over medium heat. Add the onion, ginger-garlic paste, and chile pepper. Cook until the onions are translucent, 2 to 3 minutes.

2. Add the tomato, garam masala, salt, and pepper. Mix well and cook until the tomatoes are soft, 2 to 3 minutes.

3. Stir in the whisked eggs and cook, stirring, until set, 2 to 3 minutes. Sprinkle with the cilantro and serve hot.

Paneer Makhani

PREP TIME: 15 minutes   COOK TIME: 20 minutes   TOTAL TIME: 35 minutes

Makhani sauce is a rich, creamy, and buttery tomato sauce that forms the base of this dish. Fresh, ripe tomatoes are wonderful to use for this recipe when they are in season, but canned tomato puree gives the same depth of color and flavor, so I've used that here instead. Freshly made Garam Masala (page 164) gives this dish an amazing flavor. Serve with Naan (page 108) or Basmati Rice (page 121). SERVES 6

2 tablespoons butter

1 tablespoon vegetable or canola oil

1 large onion, chopped

1½ teaspoons Ginger-Garlic Paste (page 172)

2 green chile peppers, sliced

1 tablespoon tomato paste

1 cup tomato puree

¼ teaspoon ground turmeric

1 teaspoon cayenne pepper

1½ teaspoons Garam Masala (page 164)

1 teaspoon sugar

1 teaspoon salt

1 tablespoon almond meal or ground almonds (optional)

½ cup water

2 cups paneer, store-bought or homemade (page 170), **cut into 1-inch cubes**

2 tablespoons heavy cream

1 tablespoon dried fenugreek leaves (kasoori methi)

1. Heat the butter and oil in a skillet over medium heat. Once the butter melts, add the onion, ginger-garlic paste, and chile peppers, and cook until the onions are browned around the edges, 4 to 5 minutes. Add the tomato paste and cook for 1 minute.

2. Stir in the tomato puree, turmeric, cayenne, garam masala, sugar, and salt, and cook, covered, for 5 minutes. Add the almond meal (if using) and the water, and simmer for 3 to 4 minutes.

3. Stir in the paneer and cook until heated through, 3 to 4 minutes. Finally, stir in the cream and fenugreek, and cook for 2 more minutes. Serve warm.

Tips: To make this dish vegan, use extra-firm tofu, chickpeas, and/or vegetables instead of the paneer, and use vegan butter or oil instead of the butter. Omit the cream altogether or use nondairy almond or coconut cream instead.

Palak Paneer

PREP TIME: 15 minutes   COOK TIME: 20 minutes   TOTAL TIME: 35 minutes

This dish, a rich and decadent Indian version of creamed spinach, is a popular item on most Indian restaurant menus. Traditionally, the spinach is pureed to make the curry smooth, but you can skip that step if you'd like to have some texture in the dish. I love serving this vibrant green curry with plain Naan (page 108) or Paratha (page 112). SERVES 6

1 teaspoon vegetable or canola oil

1 small onion, chopped

2 green chile peppers, sliced

2 teaspoons peeled grated fresh ginger

3 garlic cloves, chopped

1½ pounds fresh spinach, coarsely chopped

2 tablespoons Ghee (page 167) **or butter**

½ teaspoon cumin seeds

½ cup tomato puree

½ teaspoon cayenne pepper

1 teaspoon salt

2 cups paneer, store-bought or homemade (page 170), cut into 1-inch cubes

½ teaspoon Garam Masala (page 164)

2 tablespoons cream

1. Heat the oil in a large skillet over medium heat. Add the onion, chile peppers, ginger, and garlic, and cook until the onions are lightly browned around the edges, 3 to 4 minutes. Stir in the spinach and cook until wilted, 3 to 4 minutes. Turn off the heat and let the mixture cool completely.

2. Transfer the mixture to a food processor or blender and blend it into a smooth paste, adding a bit of water if needed.

3. In the same skillet over medium heat, heat the ghee or butter. Once the foaming subsides, add the cumin and cook for 30 seconds. Add the tomato puree, cayenne, and salt and cook, covered, for 2 to 3 minutes.

4. Add the spinach puree and paneer and simmer, covered, for 4 to 5 minutes. Stir in the garam masala and cream and cook until heated through, 1 to 2 minutes.

Tip: Frozen spinach is a great and convenient substitute for fresh spinach in this recipe. Use a 10-ounce box of frozen spinach instead of the chopped fresh spinach.

Egg Curry

This dish is a great example of how eggs do not have to be restricted to breakfast or brunch. My family loves eggs and are happy to eat them for any meal of the day. This egg curry is my go-to recipe when I have to make something simple and filling. I usually serve it with Basmati Rice (page 121) or Naan (page 108) and a simple salad for a filling meal. SERVES 4

1 tablespoon vegetable or
 canola oil

1 large onion,
 finely chopped

2 green chile peppers,
 halved lengthwise

3 garlic cloves,
 finely minced

1 cup tomato puree

¼ teaspoon
 cayenne pepper

¼ teaspoon ground cumin

½ teaspoon ground
 coriander

¼ teaspoon Garam Masala
 (page 164)

1 teaspoon salt

½ cup water

4 large eggs, boiled
 and peeled

2 tablespoons finely
 chopped fresh cilantro

1. Heat the oil in a medium skillet over medium heat. Add the onion, chile peppers, and garlic, and cook until the onions are lightly browned around the edges, 4 to 5 minutes. Stir in the tomato puree, cayenne, cumin, coriander, garam masala, and salt. Cover and simmer for 5 to 7 minutes.

2. Add the water and eggs and cook until heated through, 3 to 4 minutes. Stir in the cilantro and mix well. Serve hot.

Chile Paneer

PREP TIME: 15 minutes   COOK TIME: 30 minutes   TOTAL TIME: 45 minutes

Crispy batter-fried paneer is tossed in a spicy chile sauce in this fusion of Indian and Chinese cooking styles and ingredients. The sauce also has green and red bell peppers for color and crunch. Serve this with Vegetable Fried Rice (page 127) for a delicious homemade Indo-Chinese meal. SERVES 4

2 tablespoons vegetable or canola oil, plus more for deep-frying

1 teaspoon peeled grated fresh ginger

2 garlic cloves, finely minced

1 medium red onion, chopped

2 green chile peppers, halved lengthwise

1 medium green bell pepper, chopped

1 medium red bell pepper, chopped

4 scallions, chopped

2 tablespoons tomato ketchup or tomato paste

1 tablespoon low-sodium soy sauce

½ teaspoon chile-garlic sauce, store-bought

1 teaspoon white or rice vinegar

1 teaspoon salt, divided

½ teaspoon freshly ground black pepper, divided

1. Heat the oil in a large skillet over medium-high heat. Add the ginger and garlic and cook until fragrant, 30 to 45 seconds.

2. Add the onion, chile peppers, bell peppers, and scallions and cook, stirring frequently, until the veggies are crisp-tender, 4 to 5 minutes.

3. Stir in the ketchup, soy sauce, chile-garlic sauce, vinegar, ½ teaspoon of salt, and ¼ teaspoon of pepper. Mix well and cook for 2 minutes or until the mixture comes to a simmer. Cover the skillet and keep the sauce warm while you make the crispy paneer.

4. In a medium bowl, combine the flour, cornstarch, cayenne, the remaining ½ teaspoon of salt, and the remaining ¼ teaspoon of pepper. Mix well. Stir in ⅓ cup of water, adding more if needed, to make a thick, pourable batter. Add the paneer and toss gently to coat the pieces evenly.

5. Fill a medium wok or heavy-bottomed skillet 2 inches deep with oil and heat over medium-high heat to 350°F.

3 tablespoons
all-purpose flour

2 tablespoons cornstarch

½ teaspoon
cayenne pepper

⅓ cup water, plus more
if needed

2 cups paneer,
store-bought or
homemade (page 170),
cut into 1-inch cubes

6. Working in batches, gently add the batter-coated paneer to the hot oil. Cook until the coating turns golden on all sides. Use a slotted spoon to transfer the fried paneer to a paper towel–lined plate. Repeat with the remaining paneer cubes.

7. Reheat the chile sauce until simmering and add the fried paneer. Cook for 1 to 2 minutes for the flavors to mingle. Serve immediately.

Tip: The chile sauce can be made up to 2 days ahead and stored in the refrigerator in an airtight container. Make the fried paneer on the day of serving. Add it to the sauce and reheat just before serving.

Spicy Paneer Flatbread

PREP TIME: 20 minutes   **COOK TIME:** 35 minutes   **TOTAL TIME:** 55 minutes

My kids love pizza and paneer, so, this is my version of pizza with an Indian twist. Homemade Naan (page 108) is the perfect base for these flatbreads, but in case you're pressed for time, this recipe uses store-bought naan. Premade pizza crust can also work in a pinch. Drizzle with Cilantro Mint Chutney (page 134) to make this flatbread extra special. SERVES 6

1 cup paneer, store-bought or homemade (page 170), **cut into ½-inch cubes**

1 teaspoon Tandoori Masala (page 165)

1¼ teaspoons salt, divided

2 tablespoons vegetable or canola oil, divided

1 small onion, finely chopped

½ teaspoon Ginger-Garlic Paste (page 172)

1 cup tomato puree

½ teaspoon cayenne pepper

½ teaspoon Garam Masala (page 164)

1 teaspoon dried fenugreek leaves (kasoori methi)

¼ cup water

1 tablespoon heavy cream (optional)

4 naan, store-bought or homemade (page 108)

1 cup grated mozzarella cheese, divided

½ cup Cilantro-Mint Chutney (page 134), **for serving** (optional)

1. Preheat the oven to 425°F.

2. In a small bowl, combine the paneer, tandoori masala, ½ teaspoon of salt, and 1 tablespoon of oil. Mix well and set aside.

3. Heat the remaining 1 tablespoon of oil in a medium saucepan over medium heat. Add the onion and ginger-garlic paste and cook until the onion is turning lightly golden around the edges, 3 to 4 minutes. Stir in the tomato puree and cayenne and cook, covered, for 7 to 8 minutes.

4. Add the garam masala, fenugreek, remaining ¾ teaspoon of salt, and water. Simmer the mixture for 3 minutes. Finally, add the cream (if using) and cook until heated through, 2 minutes. Remove the sauce from the heat and let it cool for 10 minutes.

5. Place 1 naan on a parchment-lined baking sheet. Spread it with a thin layer of the tomato sauce, sprinkle on ¼ cup of mozzarella, and top the flatbread with one-quarter of the marinated paneer.

6. Bake for 6 to 8 minutes or until the cheese has melted. Remove from the oven, slice, and serve. Repeat with the remaining naan.

Tip: Leftover Paneer Makhani (page 39) or Paneer Tikka (page 35) makes an excellent topping for the flatbread as well.

Anda Ghotala

PREP TIME: 10 minutes   **COOK TIME:** 15 minutes   **TOTAL TIME:** 25 minutes

Ghotala means "scam" or "confusion" in Hindi, but there is nothing confusing about this delicious egg preparation. The recipe uses eggs in two different forms: boiled and scrambled. It is a popular street food in many Indian states and is served with buttered "pav" or sandwich rolls. SERVES 4

4 large eggs

2 teaspoons vegetable or canola oil

2 teaspoons butter

1 medium onion, finely chopped

1 teaspoon Ginger-Garlic Paste (page 172)

1 green chile pepper, finely chopped (optional)

3 tomatoes, chopped

¼ teaspoon ground turmeric

½ teaspoon cayenne pepper

1 teaspoon Pav Bhaji Masala (page 174)

1 teaspoon salt

¼ cup water

2 tablespoons finely chopped fresh cilantro

1. Boil 2 eggs and let them cool. Once they are cool to the touch, peel the eggs and grate them into a small bowl. Crack the remaining 2 eggs into a separate small bowl and set aside.

2. Heat the oil and butter in a medium skillet over medium heat. Add the onion, ginger-garlic paste, and chile pepper (if using) and cook until the onion is slightly browned around the edges, 3 to 4 minutes.

3. Add the tomatoes, turmeric, cayenne, pav bhaji masala, and salt, and cook until the tomatoes are mushy, 4 to 5 minutes.

4. Add the grated boiled eggs and mix until they are well-incorporated. Stir in the water and bring to a simmer. Add the cracked eggs and mix well. Cook until the eggs are scrambled and cooked through, 2 to 3 minutes. Sprinkle with the cilantro and serve hot.

Kadai Paneer

PREP TIME: 15 minutes   COOK TIME: 20 minutes   TOTAL TIME: 35 minutes

This spicy dish uses freshly made kadai masala, which provides the characteristic flavor of this curry. Make a double batch of the masala and store it in an airtight container for up to a month so you can whip up this curry in no time, whenever you want. SERVES 6

1 teaspoon
  coriander seeds

1 dry red chile pepper

1 teaspoon cumin seeds

½ teaspoon fennel seeds

2 cardamom pods

2 whole cloves

1 tablespoon vegetable oil

1 tablespoon butter

1 medium onion,
  finely chopped

2 green chile peppers, sliced

1 teaspoon Ginger-Garlic
  Paste (page 172)

2 medium tomatoes,
  chopped

1 tablespoon tomato paste

¼ teaspoon ground
  turmeric

½ teaspoon cayenne pepper

½ teaspoon Garam Masala
  (page 164)

1 teaspoon salt

1 cup water

1 medium green or red bell
  pepper, chopped

2 cups paneer,
  store-bought or
  homemade (page 170),
  cut into ½-inch cubes

3 tablespoons heavy cream

1 teaspoon dried
  fenugreek leaves

1. In a small skillet over medium-low heat, dry roast the coriander, chile pepper, cumin, fennel, cardamom, and cloves until the spices are aromatic and a shade darker. Let the spices cool, and grind them to a fine powder in a spice grinder or with a mortar and pestle. Set aside.

2. Heat the oil and butter in a medium skillet over medium heat. Add the onion, chile peppers, and ginger-garlic paste, and cook until the onion is lightly browned around the edges, 4 to 5 minutes. Add the tomatoes, tomato paste, turmeric, cayenne, garam masala, and salt. Mix well, cover, and cook for 5 minutes or until the tomatoes turn mushy.

3. Stir in the water, bell pepper, and paneer. Bring the mixture to a boil over medium-high heat. Lower the heat and simmer until the peppers are crisp-tender, 6 to 8 minutes.

4. Whisk in the cream, spice powder, and fenugreek. Cook until heated through, 2 to 3 minutes. Serve hot or warm.

Kadhi

PREP TIME: 10 minutes   COOK TIME: 15 minutes   TOTAL TIME: 25 minutes

Yogurt-based dishes are very popular in India. Each region has its own version of kadhi based on the local spices and ingredients. This recipe is a Punjabi version that has become quite popular in Indian restaurants. SERVES 4

1 cup Yogurt (page 168)

3 tablespoons chickpea flour (besan)

½ teaspoon cayenne pepper

½ teaspoon Garam Masala (page 164)

1 teaspoon salt

1 cup water

2 teaspoons vegetable or canola oil

½ teaspoon mustard seeds

⅛ teaspoon fenugreek seeds

⅛ teaspoon asafetida (hing)

1 dried red chile pepper, broken

6 curry leaves

1 small onion, finely chopped

1 green chile pepper, halved lengthwise

1 teaspoon peeled grated fresh ginger

2 garlic cloves, finely minced

2 tablespoons finely chopped fresh cilantro

1. In a small mixing bowl, combine the yogurt, chickpea flour, cayenne, garam masala, and salt. Whisk well to combine. Add the water and whisk again until completely smooth. Set aside.

2. Heat the oil in a medium saucepan over medium heat. Add the mustard seeds and fenugreek seeds, and once the seeds start to splutter, add the asafetida, red chile pepper, and curry leaves. Cook for 30 to 45 seconds.

3. Stir in the onion, green chile pepper, ginger, and garlic, and cook until the onion turns translucent, 3 to 4 minutes.

4. Slowly stir in the yogurt mixture while whisking constantly. Lower the heat to medium-low and simmer for 6 to 8 minutes, or until the mixture thickens. Sprinkle with the cilantro and serve with rice.

Egg and Lentil Curry

PREP TIME: 20 minutes   COOK TIME: 40 minutes   TOTAL TIME: 1 hour

This hearty and comforting dish gives you a double dose of protein from the eggs and lentils. It is great for either lunch or dinner. You can substitute mung beans (moong dal) for the brown lentils, or you can use canned lentils instead; just make sure to rinse and drain them before using. Serve this curry with plain Naan (page 108) or over Basmati Rice (page 121). SERVES 6

½ cup brown lentils (whole masoor dal), rinsed and drained

2 cups vegetable broth or water

6 large eggs

4½ cups water, divided

2 tablespoons vegetable or canola oil

3 whole cloves

4 black peppercorns

1 medium onion, finely chopped

2 green chile peppers, halved lengthwise

1 cup tomato puree

1 teaspoon salt

½ teaspoon cayenne pepper

½ teaspoon Garam Masala (page 164)

½ teaspoon freshly ground black pepper

2 tablespoons finely chopped fresh cilantro

1. In a medium saucepan, combine the lentils and broth. Bring the mixture to a boil, lower the heat, cover, and cook for 25 to 30 minutes, or until the lentils are tender and all the broth has been absorbed.

2. While the lentils are cooking, in a separate medium saucepan, bring the eggs and 4¼ cups water to a boil. Once the water comes to a boil, turn off the heat, cover the pan, and set it aside for 12 minutes. Drain the water and place the boiled eggs in a bowl with ice cubes. Once they are cool enough to handle, peel the eggs and cut them in half lengthwise. Set aside.

3. Heat the oil in a large skillet over medium heat. Add the cloves and peppercorns and cook for 30 seconds. Add the onion and chile peppers and cook until the onion is lightly browned around the edges, 4 to 5 minutes. Stir in the tomato puree, salt, cayenne, garam masala, and black pepper. Cook for 5 minutes.

4. Add the lentils and the remaining ¼ cup of water, mix well, and add the eggs. Cover and cook for 10 minutes. Turn off the heat and sprinkle with the cilantro.

Dahi Baingan
(Eggplant in Yogurt Sauce)

PREP TIME: 10 minutes   COOK TIME: 20 minutes   TOTAL TIME: 30 minutes

Yogurt is used widely in Indian cooking, and in this recipe, it is the star of the show, creating a creamy, delicious sauce that even the pickiest of eaters will adore. Make sure to use tender eggplant to get the best flavor in this dish. The technique of adding chickpea flour to yogurt before heating stabilizes the yogurt and prevents it from curdling. Okra or even chickpeas can be substituted for eggplant to make equally delicious yogurt-based curries. Serve with Methi Roti (page 110) or Basmati Rice (page 121). SERVES 4

1 cup Yogurt (page 168)

2 teaspoons chickpea flour (besan)

2 tablespoons vegetable or canola oil

½ teaspoon cumin seeds

2 teaspoons peeled grated fresh ginger

2 garlic cloves, finely minced

1 small globe eggplant or 2 Japanese eggplants, chopped

¼ teaspoon ground turmeric

1 teaspoon ground coriander

1 teaspoon cayenne pepper

1 teaspoon salt

3 tablespoons finely chopped fresh cilantro

1. In a small bowl, whisk the yogurt with the chickpea flour until well combined and completely smooth. Set aside.

2. Heat the oil in a large skillet over medium heat. Add the cumin seeds, ginger, and garlic, and cook for 1 to 2 minutes or until fragrant. Add the eggplant, mix well, and cook, covered, for 5 to 6 minutes. Add the turmeric, coriander, cayenne, and salt. Mix well and cook until the eggplant is tender, 4 to 5 minutes.

3. Stir in the yogurt mixture and simmer for 2 to 3 minutes. If the mixture looks too dry, add ¼ cup of water and bring to a simmer. Serve hot.

Egg Pulao

PREP TIME: 20 minutes, plus 30 minutes to soak
COOK TIME: 30 minutes   TOTAL TIME: 1 hour 20 minutes

This delicious one-pot dish is easy enough to make on a weeknight and fancy enough to serve to your friends and family. Fresh herbs and whole spices add a lot of flavor to the dish and complement the eggs and rice beautifully. Serve with Raita (page 169) or plain Yogurt (page 168). **SERVES 6**

1½ cups basmati rice, washed and drained

3 cups water

6 large eggs, boiled and peeled

2 tablespoons canola oil

1 (1-inch) piece cinnamon stick

3 whole cloves

3 cardamom pods

1 bay leaf

1 teaspoon cumin seeds

1 large onion, thinly sliced

2 green chile peppers, sliced

1½ teaspoons Ginger-Garlic Paste (page 172)

3 medium tomatoes, chopped

¼ cup mint leaves, chopped

¼ cup chopped cilantro

¼ teaspoon ground turmeric

1 teaspoon cayenne pepper

1½ teaspoons salt

½ cup green peas

1 tablespoon freshly squeezed lemon juice

1. Soak the rice in the water for 30 minutes. Using a sharp knife, make a 2-inch slit along the length of each egg. Set the eggs aside.

2. Heat the oil in a large skillet over medium heat. Add the cinnamon, cloves, cardamom, bay leaf, and cumin. Cook for 1 minute or until fragrant. Add the onion, chile peppers, and ginger-garlic paste, and cook until the onion turns translucent, 3 to 4 minutes. Add the tomatoes and cook for an additional 3 to 4 minutes or until mushy.

3. Stir in the mint, cilantro, turmeric, cayenne, and salt. Cook for 2 minutes. Add the soaked rice along with the water, eggs, peas, and lemon juice. Mix gently and bring to a boil on high heat. Lower the heat, cover the pan, and cook until all the water is absorbed and the rice is cooked through, 15 to 20 minutes. Gently fluff the rice with a fork and serve hot.

Paneer Bhurji

PREP TIME: 10 minutes   **COOK TIME:** 20 minutes   **TOTAL TIME:** 30 minutes

Paneer bhurji is a lacto-vegetarian's version of Anda Bhurji (page 38). Crumbled paneer has a texture similar to scrambled eggs and works beautifully in this recipe. I added vegetables for color and to make it more substantial. Serve with toast for breakfast, or wrap it in Methi Roti (page 110) or Naan (page 108) and enjoy it for lunch. SERVES 4

1 tablespoon vegetable or canola oil

½ teaspoon cumin seeds

1 teaspoon peeled grated fresh ginger

1 or 2 green chile peppers, finely chopped

1 small red onion, finely chopped

1 small red bell pepper, finely chopped

1 medium tomato, chopped

2 cups paneer, store-bought or homemade (page 170), grated or crumbled

½ teaspoon Garam Masala (page 164)

¾ teaspoon salt

2 tablespoons finely chopped fresh cilantro

1. Heat the oil in a large skillet over medium heat. Add the cumin and cook until it is fragrant, about 30 seconds. Add the ginger, chile peppers, onion, and bell pepper, and cook until the veggies are crisp-tender, 4 to 5 minutes. Stir in the tomato and cook until it is soft, 2 to 3 minutes.

2. Add the paneer, garam masala, and salt, and mix well. Lower the heat, cover, and cook for 6 to 8 minutes. Sprinkle with the cilantro and mix well. Serve hot.

Tip: To make this dish vegan, use extra-firm tofu instead of paneer and follow the recipe as written.

Paneer Do Pyaza

PREP TIME: 15 minutes   **COOK TIME:** 30 minutes   **TOTAL TIME:** 45 minutes

Do pyaza means "two onions" in Hindi. The onions in this recipe are used in different forms, one finely chopped and the other cubed, to provide a nice textural difference in the curry. The finely chopped onions melt into the tomato sauce while the bigger chunks give some bite to the dish. The spices used here complement the onion flavor beautifully. Okra or mushrooms can be substituted for paneer. Serve with Naan (page 108) or Paratha (page 112). **SERVES 4**

1 tablespoon vegetable or canola oil

½ teaspoon cumin seeds

2 medium onions, 1 cut into chunks, 1 finely chopped

1 teaspoon Ginger-Garlic Paste (page 172)

2 tablespoons tomato paste

¼ teaspoon ground turmeric

1 teaspoon cayenne pepper

½ teaspoon ground cumin

½ teaspoon ground coriander

½ teaspoon Garam Masala (page 164)

1 teaspoon salt

½ cup water

2 cups paneer, store-bought or homemade (page 170), **cut into 1-inch cubes**

2 teaspoons dried fenugreek leaves (kasoori methi)

2 tablespoons almond meal

1. Heat the oil in a medium skillet over medium heat. Add the cumin seeds and, once they start to splutter, add the finely chopped onion. Cook until the onion starts turning lightly browned around the edges, 3 to 4 minutes. Stir in the ginger-garlic paste and cook for 1 minute.

2. Add the tomato paste and cook for 1 to 2 minutes. Add the turmeric, cayenne, ground cumin, coriander, garam masala, and salt. Stir in the water and bring the mixture to a simmer.

3. Add the onion chunks and paneer, and simmer the mixture until the onion is crisp-tender, 3 to 4 minutes. Finally, stir in the fenugreek and almond meal. Mix well and serve.

Bhindi Masala page 58

4
Stir-Fried Vegetable Mains

Gobi Aloo

PREP TIME: 20 minutes   COOK TIME: 30 minutes   TOTAL TIME: 50 minutes

Cauliflower (gobi) and potato (aloo) is a classic combination and is one of the popular dishes served in Indian restaurants. This version is flavored with spices and is easy to make at home. Parcooking the veggies before adding the onion-tomato sauce ensures that they retain their shape and don't turn mushy. **SERVES 6**

1½ teaspoons **Garam Masala** (page 164)

½ teaspoon **ground turmeric**

1½ teaspoons **salt**

1 teaspoon **dried mango powder (amchur)**

1 teaspoon **cayenne pepper**

2 tablespoons **chickpea flour (besan)**

3 tablespoons **vegetable or canola oil, divided**

2 medium **potatoes, peeled and diced into 1-inch cubes**

1 small head **cauliflower, cut into 2-inch florets**

1 teaspoon **cumin seeds**

1 medium **onion, chopped**

1½ teaspoons **Ginger-Garlic Paste** (page 172)

2 medium **tomatoes, chopped**

1 teaspoon **dried fenugreek leaves (kasoori methi), crushed**

½ teaspoon **red pepper flakes** (optional)

3 tablespoons **finely chopped fresh cilantro**

1. In a small bowl, combine the garam masala, turmeric, salt, mango powder, cayenne, and chickpea flour. Mix well and set aside.

2. Heat 1 tablespoon of oil in a large skillet over medium heat. Add the potatoes, cover, and cook, stirring occasionally, until they are fork-tender, 8 to 10 minutes. Transfer to a large plate. In the same skillet, heat 1 tablespoon of oil and sauté the cauliflower until tender, another 8 to 10 minutes. Transfer the cauliflower to the same plate.

3. Heat the remaining 1 tablespoon of oil in the skillet over medium heat. Add the cumin seeds and cook for 30 seconds or until fragrant. Add the onion and ginger-garlic paste and cook until the onion is slightly browned around the edges. Stir in the tomatoes and cook until the tomatoes are soft, 3 to 4 minutes.

4. Return the potatoes and cauliflower to the skillet. Stir in the spice mix, fenugreek, and red pepper flakes (if using). Gently toss and cook, covered, for 4 to 5 minutes. If the curry looks too dry, add 2 tablespoons of water. Sprinkle with the cilantro and mix well. Serve hot.

Baingan Bharta

PREP TIME: 10 minutes   **COOK TIME:** 45 minutes   **TOTAL TIME:** 55 minutes

This smoky eggplant dish is a delicious addition to any meal. Traditionally, eggplants are cooked directly on the hot coals of a clay oven known as a tandoor. But similar flavors can be achieved by cooking them on a gas burner, in a hot oven, or even on an outdoor grill. I am a big fan of the smoky roasted eggplant flavor, which is enhanced in this dish with the use of smoky ground cumin. Serve with Methi Roti (page 110), plain Naan (page 108), or plain Basmati Rice (page 121). SERVES 4

1 large globe eggplant or 4 small Italian eggplants

3 tablespoons vegetable or canola oil

1 teaspoon cumin seeds

1 medium onion, finely chopped

2 green chile peppers, finely chopped

1 teaspoon Ginger-Garlic Paste (page 172)

2 medium tomatoes, chopped

½ teaspoon cayenne pepper

1 teaspoon salt

½ teaspoon Garam Masala (page 164)

2 tablespoons finely chopped fresh cilantro

1. Preheat the oven to 450°F. Line a baking sheet with aluminum foil.

2. Pierce the eggplant with a fork to allow steam to escape. Place it on the prepared baking sheet and bake for 20 to 25 minutes, or until the eggplant is very tender and the skin starts to peel off. Transfer the eggplant to a medium bowl and cover with a lid or plastic wrap for 10 to 15 minutes. Remove the stem and skin and coarsely chop or mash the flesh. Set aside.

3. Heat the oil in a medium skillet over medium heat. Add the cumin seeds and, once they start to splutter, add the onion, chile peppers, and ginger-garlic paste and cook until the onion is translucent, 3 to 4 minutes.

4. Stir in the tomatoes, cayenne, and salt, and cook until the tomatoes are mushy, 3 to 4 minutes. Add the cooked eggplant and garam masala and cook for 4 for 5 minutes. Sprinkle with the cilantro and serve warm.

Tip: To cook the eggplant on an outdoor grill, place it on the grill grate, cover, and cook, turning occasionally, until the eggplant is tender and charred all over. Proceed with the recipe.

Bhindi Masala (Okra-Tomato Curry)

PREP TIME: 15 minutes   COOK TIME: 30 minutes   TOTAL TIME: 45 minutes

Growing up, we were told that eating okra would make us smart, especially in math. I do not think there is any scientific evidence behind that, but okra sure is delicious in any dish, be it Okra Fries (page 23) or this simple, every-day curry. Okra tends to turn slimy when cooked. To avoid that, make sure that the okra is washed and dried completely. Lay the pods out on a kitchen towel before chopping them. Also, sautéing the okra before adding it to the tomato mixture ensures that it does not turn mushy and that it holds its shape in the final dish. Serve with Basmati Rice (page 121) or plain Naan (page 108). SERVES 4

1 pound okra, washed and drained well

3 tablespoons vegetable or canola oil, divided

1 teaspoon cumin seeds

1 medium onion, finely chopped

1 teaspoon Ginger-Garlic Paste (page 172)

2 medium tomatoes, chopped

¼ teaspoon ground turmeric

¾ teaspoon cayenne pepper

1 teaspoon ground coriander

1 teaspoon dried mango powder (amchur)

1 teaspoon salt

¼ cup water

1 teaspoon Garam Masala (page 164)

1 tablespoon finely chopped fresh cilantro

1. Lay the okra on a kitchen towel and pat them dry. Trim the ends and cut them into ½-inch pieces.

2. Heat 2 tablespoons of oil in a large skillet over medium heat. Add the okra and sauté for 6 to 8 minutes, stirring occasionally. Do not stir the okra too often, because that will make them slimy. Once the okra is lightly browned on all sides and slightly tender, transfer it to a plate and set it aside.

3. In the same skillet, heat the remaining 1 tablespoon of oil. Add the cumin seeds and, once they start to splutter, add the onion and cook until it's lightly brown around the edges, 3 to 4 minutes. Add the tomatoes, turmeric, cayenne, coriander, mango powder, and salt. Cook until the tomatoes turn mushy, 3 to 4 minutes.

4. Stir in the water and bring the mixture to a boil. Return the sautéed okra to the skillet and simmer for 10 minutes or until the okra is completely cooked through. Finally, stir in the garam masala and chopped cilantro. Serve hot or warm.

Tip: If fresh okra is not available, frozen chopped okra can be used. Do not thaw before adding it to the curry, as this will make the dish slimy.

Arbi Sabzi (Crispy Taro Root)

PREP TIME: 10 minutes   **COOK TIME:** 30 minutes   **TOTAL TIME:** 40 minutes

Arbi, or taro root, is gnarly and hairy and is usually seen next to root vegetables in the grocery store. Don't let its looks intimidate you; it is a delicious vegetable, particularly in this recipe. This crispy taro root is my kids' favorite dish and I make it at least once a week. Serve with Basmati Rice (page 121) and your favorite dal. SERVES 4

10 to 12 medium taro root (arbi), peeled and cut into 1-inch dice

2 tablespoons vegetable or canola oil

1 teaspoon cayenne pepper

¼ teaspoon ground turmeric

1 teaspoon salt

½ teaspoon Garam Masala (page 164)

¼ teaspoon dried mango powder (amchur)

1 tablespoon chickpea flour (besan)

1. In a medium saucepan over medium-high heat, combine the taro with enough water to cover. Bring to a boil, reduce the heat to low, cover, and simmer until the pieces are fork-tender, 10 minutes. Drain and set aside.

2. Heat the oil in a large nonstick skillet over medium heat. Add the drained taro pieces and cook, stirring occasionally, until they start to turn crispy and golden on all sides, 10 to 12 minutes. Add the cayenne, turmeric, salt, garam masala, mango powder, and chickpea flour. Mix well to evenly coat the taro with the spices. Cook for another 3 to 5 minutes or until the taro is evenly crispy on all sides. Serve immediately.

Tip: The hairy outer skin of taro root can cause itchiness in some people with sensitive skin; use disposable gloves if you are not sure. Also, do not eat taro raw or undercooked.

Eggplant with Onion Sauté

PREP TIME: 10 minutes   **COOK TIME:** 20 minutes   **TOTAL TIME:** 30 minutes

Eggplant is a wonderfully versatile vegetable and tastes great either roasted, as in Baingan Bharta (page 57), or sautéed, as in this dish. Baby eggplants found in Indian or Asian stores are less watery and have fewer seeds than globe eggplants. They lend the best taste to this curry, but medium-size Chinese or Japanese eggplants can also be used. For extra color and variety, cook diced potato or bell peppers along with the eggplant until tender. Serve this dish with Basmati Rice (page 121) or plain Paratha (page 112). SERVES 4

10 to 12 baby eggplants or 2 medium Chinese or Japanese eggplants

2 tablespoons vegetable or canola oil

½ teaspoon cumin seeds

1 medium red onion, thinly sliced

1 or 2 green chile peppers, sliced

2 garlic cloves, finely minced

¼ teaspoon ground turmeric

½ teaspoon cayenne pepper

1 teaspoon salt

½ cup green peas

2 tablespoons finely chopped fresh cilantro

1. Remove the crowns from the eggplants, halve the eggplants lengthwise, and cut them into 1-inch strips. Place in a bowl filled with water. Set aside.

2. Heat the oil in a large skillet over medium heat. Add the cumin seeds and, once they start to change color, add the onion, chile peppers, and garlic. Cook for 3 to 4 minutes or until the onion is soft and turning brown around the edges.

3. Drain the eggplants and add them to the skillet along with the turmeric, cayenne, and salt. Cover and cook until the eggplant is soft, 10 minutes. Add the peas and cook until they are tender, 3 to 4 minutes. Sprinkle with the cilantro and serve hot or warm.

Bharli Karela (Stuffed Bitter Melon)

PREP TIME: 15 minutes, plus 30 minutes to marinate
COOK TIME: 30 minutes   TOTAL TIME: 1 hour 15 minutes

As the name suggests, bitter melon is indeed bitter. But using ingredients that complement the bitter flavor makes this vegetable one of the most beloved in India. I marinate chopped bitter melon in salt and lemon juice to remove some of the bitterness; then the pieces are rinsed, drained, and cooked. In this recipe, bitter melons are stuffed with a spiced onion mixture and then cooked until toasted. Serve with Basmati Rice (page 121) and your favorite dal. SERVES 4

4 medium bitter melons

1 tablespoon freshly squeezed lemon juice

1½ teaspoons salt, divided

3 tablespoons vegetable or canola oil, divided

1 medium onion, finely chopped

1 teaspoon Ginger-Garlic Paste (page 172)

1 teaspoon ground coriander

1 teaspoon ground cumin

1½ tablespoons chickpea flour (besan)

1 teaspoon cayenne pepper

1 teaspoon dry mango powder (amchur)

1. Use a paring knife to lightly scrape off the bitter melon skins. Make a deep slit in the middle of each melon, and remove and reserve the seeds. Place the bitter melon in a small bowl, add the lemon juice and 1 teaspoon of salt, toss well, and set aside to marinate for at least 30 minutes. Squeeze the melons to remove any bitterness, then wash them under running water and squeeze out any extra water.

2. Heat 1 tablespoon of oil in a skillet over medium heat. Add the onion and ginger-garlic paste and cook until the onion turns translucent, 3 to 4 minutes. Stir in the coriander, cumin, chickpea flour, cayenne, mango powder, the remaining ½ teaspoon of salt, and the reserved bitter melon seeds. Mix well and cook for 2 more minutes. Let the stuffing cool slightly.

3. Fill each hollowed-out bitter melon with 1 to 2 tablespoons of stuffing and tie tightly with kitchen string to make sure the stuffing does not spill out. Reserve any leftover stuffing.

4. Heat the remaining 2 tablespoons of oil in a medium skillet over medium-low heat. Place the stuffed bitter melons in the skillet and cook, stirring occasionally, until the bitter melon is tender and toasted on all sides, 12 to 15 minutes. Add the reserved stuffing and ¼ cup of water. Simmer until the sauce thickens, about 10 minutes. Serve warm.

Aloo Besan Subzi (Potato Curry with Chickpea Flour)

PREP TIME: 15 minutes   **COOK TIME:** 45 minutes   **TOTAL TIME:** 1 hour

Potatoes turn up in many dishes in India, such as samosas, stuffed paratha, and many more. This ginger-flavored potato curry has a thick, creamy base. It's a perfect side dish to serve with Dosa (page 118), Poori (page 120) or plain Basmati Rice (page 121). **SERVES 4**

3 medium potatoes, peeled and diced

1 tablespoon vegetable or canola oil

½ teaspoon mustard seeds

½ teaspoon cumin seeds

1 tablespoon peeled grated fresh ginger

2 green chile peppers, finely chopped

4 curry leaves

1 medium onion, thinly sliced

¼ teaspoon ground turmeric

1 tablespoon chickpea flour (besan)

1¼ cups water

1 teaspoon salt

1. In a medium saucepan over high heat, combine the potatoes and enough water to cover them. Bring to a boil, then lower the heat and simmer until the potatoes are tender, 10 to 12 minutes. Drain well and return the potatoes to the pan. Mash them and set aside.

2. Heat the oil in a skillet over medium heat. Add the mustard seeds and cumin seeds and, once the seeds start to splutter, add the ginger, chile peppers, and curry leaves, and cook for 30 seconds. Next, add the onion and cook until translucent, 3 to 4 minutes.

3. Add the mashed potatoes and mix well. Stir in the turmeric and chickpea flour and cook for 30 minutes. Add the water and salt and bring the mixture to a simmer. Cook until the mixture has thickened. Curry thickens as it cools, so make sure to adjust the consistency accordingly. Serve warm.

Tindora Subzi (Ivy Gourd Sauté)

PREP TIME: 15 minutes   **COOK TIME:** 20 minutes   **TOTAL TIME:** 35 minutes

Ivy gourd (tindora in Hindi) looks like a mini cucumber, about 3 inches long. It is available throughout the year in Indian grocery stores. Look for blemish-free, firm, fresh-looking ivy gourds. They are also sold chopped and frozen. This flavorful sauté is quick and easy to make for any weeknight and can be served with plain Basmati Rice (page 121) and any dal from chapter 5. SERVES 4

2 tablespoons vegetable or canola oil

½ teaspoon cumin seeds

1 medium onion, thinly sliced

1 teaspoon Ginger-Garlic Paste (page 172)

1 pound ivy gourd (tindora), washed, trimmed, and cut into thin slices

¼ teaspoon ground turmeric

1 teaspoon salt

½ teaspoon cayenne pepper

½ teaspoon ground cumin

¼ teaspoon ground coriander

1. Heat the oil in a large skillet over medium heat. Add the cumin seeds and cook until they change color slightly, about 30 seconds. Add the onion and ginger-garlic paste and cook until the onion is translucent, 3 to 4 minutes.

2. Add the ivy gourd, turmeric, and salt. Mix well, cover, and cook, stirring occasionally, until the ivy gourd is tender, 10 to 12 minutes. Stir in the cayenne, cumin, and coriander. Cook for 2 more minutes. Serve hot or warm.

Gajar Methi Subzi (Carrot and Fenugreek Sauté)

PREP TIME: 10 minutes   **COOK TIME:** 15 minutes   **TOTAL TIME:** 25 minutes

This simple stir-fry is a colorful and easy-to-make dish that goes well with all Indian meals. Traditionally, this dish is made with young fenugreek leaves (methi) and fresh bright orange carrots (gajar) that are available in winter, but you can make it all year round. You can usually find fresh fenugreek leaves in Indian groceries throughout the year, and fresh carrots are available anytime. Serve with Khichdi (page 122) and Raita (page 169) for a simple and wholesome meal. **SERVES 4**

1 tablespoon vegetable or canola oil

1 teaspoon cumin seeds

4 medium carrots, peeled and diced

1 green chile pepper, finely chopped

¼ teaspoon ground turmeric

1 teaspoon salt

1 cup fenugreek leaves (methi)

½ teaspoon cayenne pepper

2 teaspoons freshly squeezed lemon juice

1. Heat the oil in a skillet over medium heat. Add the cumin seeds and cook for 30 seconds. Add the carrots, chile pepper, turmeric, and salt. Mix well, cover, and cook until the carrots are fork-tender, 6 to 8 minutes.

2. Stir in the fenugreek leaves and cayenne, and cook until the leaves wilt, 3 to 4 minutes. Taste and adjust the seasoning. Turn off the heat, add the lemon juice, and mix well. Serve hot.

Tips: To prep methi, pluck the leaves and tender stems from the bunch, wash them thoroughly, and then coarsely chop them. Frozen chopped methi is very convenient to use in this recipe, or fresh dill leaves can be used instead of fenugreek leaves. Dill has a distinct flavor that pairs well with carrot.

Masala Cabbage

PREP TIME: 15 minutes   **COOK TIME:** 15 minutes   **TOTAL TIME:** 30 minutes

Cabbage can sometimes be regarded as boring and bland, but when served this way, cabbage is anything but boring. This crowd favorite from North India is flavored with a wonderful blend of spices. I sometimes use store-bought coleslaw mix, which is essentially shredded cabbage and carrots, to save time. Serve with Basmati Rice (page 121) or plain Paratha (page 112). SERVES 4

2 tablespoons vegetable or canola oil

1 teaspoon cumin seeds

1 medium onion, chopped

2 teaspoons peeled grated fresh ginger

2 garlic cloves, finely minced

¼ teaspoon ground turmeric

1 pound cabbage, finely shredded

1 teaspoon ground coriander

1½ teaspoons ground cumin

½ teaspoon chili powder

¼ teaspoon ground pepper

1 teaspoon salt

1. Heat the oil in a large skillet over medium heat. Add the cumin seeds and, once they start to change color, add the onion, ginger, garlic, and turmeric, and cook until the onion turns translucent, 2 to 3 minutes.

2. Add the cabbage and mix well to evenly coat the leaves with the onion mixture. Stir in the coriander, cumin, chili powder, pepper, and salt. Cover and cook for 8 to 10 minutes, stirring occasionally, until the cabbage is tender and soft. If the cabbage starts to stick to the bottom or the mixture starts to get dry, stir in 1 to 2 tablespoons of water. Serve hot.

Tip: Brussels sprouts can be used instead of cabbage in this recipe. Trim and discard the bases and any loose or yellow outer leaves, then thinly slice the sprouts and use.

Stuffed Bell Peppers with Aloo

PREP TIME: 10 minutes   COOK TIME: 45 minutes   TOTAL TIME: 55 minutes

My mom used to make this stuffed pepper recipe quite often when we were growing up. I get excited when I see small bell peppers at the grocery store because they are great for stuffing and perfectly portion controlled, but larger peppers can be halved and stuffed to make this dish. Serve with Basmati Rice (page 121) and your favorite dal. SERVES 4

2 medium potatoes, peeled and chopped

2 tablespoons vegetable or canola oil, divided

½ teaspoon mustard seeds

½ teaspoon cumin seeds

1 small onion, chopped

¼ teaspoon ground turmeric

½ teaspoon cayenne pepper

1 teaspoon Garam Masala (page 164)

1½ teaspoons salt, divided

4 small bell peppers, cored, with seeds and stems discarded

1. In a saucepan over medium-high heat, combine the potatoes with enough water to cover them. Bring to a boil, then lower the heat and cook for 8 to 10 minutes or until the potatoes are tender. Drain the potatoes well and transfer them to a bowl. Mash and set aside.

2. Heat 1 tablespoon of oil in a skillet over medium heat. Add the mustard seeds and cumin seeds and, once the seeds start to splutter, add the onion and cook until it turns translucent, 3 to 4 minutes. Add the mashed potato, turmeric, cayenne, garam masala, and 1 teaspoon of salt, and mix well. Cook for 3 to 4 minutes for the flavors to mingle. Remove from the heat and cool for 5 minutes.

3. Using a spoon, stuff the cored peppers with the potato mixture.

4. Heat the remaining 1 tablespoon of oil in a wide skillet over medium heat and place the stuffed peppers in the pan. Cover and cook, turning the peppers occasionally to cook evenly on all sides, until tender, 10 to 12 minutes. Sprinkle with the remaining ½ teaspoon of salt. Serve warm.

Tip: My mom used to make this dish with green bell peppers, but you can create a beautiful presentation by using any color or combination of colors.

Bell Pepper Stir-Fry with Chickpea Flour

PREP TIME: 10 minutes   COOK TIME: 15 minutes   TOTAL TIME: 25 minutes

This is one of my favorite stir-fries to make when pressed for time. It comes together in less than half an hour and uses mostly pantry ingredients. Traditionally, green bell peppers are used in this dish, but feel free to use any color peppers. Chickpea flour adds a nice nutty flavor and forms a crumbly toasted coating around the peppers. It is important to cook out the rawness in the flour, so take the time to toast it well before turning off the heat. Serve with Basmati Rice (page 121) or plain Paratha (page 112). SERVES 4

2 tablespoons vegetable or canola oil

1 teaspoon mustard seeds

1 teaspoon cumin seeds

3 medium bell peppers, seeded and chopped

½ teaspoon cayenne pepper

½ teaspoon Garam Masala (page 164)

2 tablespoons chickpea flour (besan)

1 teaspoon salt

1. Heat the oil in a skillet over medium heat. Add the mustard seeds and cumin seeds and cook for 30 seconds or until the seeds start to splutter. Add the bell peppers, cover the pan, and cook until the peppers are tender, 8 minutes.

2. Stir in the cayenne, garam masala, chickpea flour, and salt. Mix well to coat the peppers with the spices. Cook for 3 to 4 minutes, or until the chickpea flour is toasted and smells aromatic. Serve right away.

Tips: Green beans, eggplant, or cabbage can be used instead of peppers in this dish. Follow the recipe as written, but adjust the cooking time according to the vegetable used.

Green Bean Sauté

PREP TIME: 15 minutes   COOK TIME: 20 minutes   TOTAL TIME: 35 minutes

Some people might regard snipping and chopping fresh green beans as a chore, but I enjoy the snapping and their fresh smell. This is my mother-in-law's recipe that I have tweaked just a little. It is a simple, every-day curry that is slightly spicy and easy to make. Serve with Basmati Rice (page 121) and your favorite dal. SERVES 4

1 tablespoon vegetable or canola oil

½ teaspoon mustard seeds

½ teaspoon cumin seeds

1 medium onion, chopped

1 pound green beans, cut into ½-inch pieces

½ teaspoon cayenne pepper

1 teaspoon dry mango powder (amchur)

½ teaspoon ground cumin

1 teaspoon salt

¼ cup water

2 tablespoons finely chopped fresh cilantro

1. Heat the oil in a large skillet over medium heat. Add the mustard seeds and cumin seeds and cook until the seeds start to splutter, 30 to 45 seconds. Add the onion and cook until it starts to lightly brown around the edges, 4 minutes.

2. Stir in the green beans, cayenne, mango powder, cumin, salt, and water. Mix well, cover, and cook, stirring occasionally, until the beans are tender, 10 to 12 minutes. Most of the water should have evaporated by this time. If not, then let the water cook away. Sprinkle with the cilantro and serve hot.

Tips: Feel free to add Garam Masala (page 164) to give more flavor to this simple curry. Frozen cut green beans can be used instead of fresh. No need to add water if using frozen beans, as they release enough water to cook the dish.

Spicy Corn Stir-Fry

PREP TIME: 10 minutes   **COOK TIME:** 15 minutes   **TOTAL TIME:** 25 minutes

This is one of my favorite dishes to make with fresh corn when it is at its seasonal peak because it adds a juicy, sweet bite to this simple stir-fry. But frozen corn kernels work well, too. Chaat masala adds a spicy, refreshing tang. This dish is colorful, quick, easy to make, and can be served as a side dish with any Indian meal. Or try adding it as a topping to a rice bowl made with Basmati Rice (page 121), Rajma Masala (page 83), and Raita (page 169). SERVES 4

1 tablespoon vegetable or
 canola oil

1 teaspoon cumin seeds

2 dried red chile
 peppers, broken

1 teaspoon peeled grated
 fresh ginger

2 garlic cloves,
 finely minced

1 medium red
 onion, chopped

1 medium red or green bell
 pepper, diced

4 scallions, chopped

1 or 2 green chile
 peppers, sliced

2 cups corn kernels, fresh
 or frozen

1 medium tomato, chopped

¾ teaspoon salt

½ teaspoon Chaat Masala
 (page 166)

1. Heat the oil in a large skillet over medium heat. Add the cumin seeds and red chile peppers and cook for 30 seconds or until they change color slightly. Add the ginger and garlic and cook, stirring, for 1 minute or until fragrant.

2. Add the onion, bell pepper, scallions, and green chile peppers. Stir-fry until the veggies are crisp-tender, 4 to 5 minutes. Stir in the corn and tomato and cook for 3 to 4 minutes, or until the tomato is tender but not mushy. Season with the salt and chaat masala and cook for 1 more minute. Serve hot.

Leafy Greens Stir-Fry

PREP TIME: 10 minutes   COOK TIME: 15 minutes   TOTAL TIME: 25 minutes

This is a versatile recipe that can be used to cook any leafy green. I have used kale here, but feel free to use Swiss chard, spinach, mustard, or collard greens, or a combination of these. Frozen chopped greens would also work well. Serve with Paratha (page 112) or Basmati Rice (page 121) and your favorite dal for a wholesome meal. SERVES 4

1 tablespoon vegetable or canola oil

½ teaspoon mustard seeds

1 teaspoon split black lentils (urad dal)

2 dried red chile peppers, halved

1 large onion, chopped

2 green chile peppers, sliced

1 bunch kale, chopped (4 cups)

½ teaspoon salt

2 tablespoons fresh or dry grated unsweetened coconut

1. Heat the oil in a large skillet over medium heat. Add the mustard seeds, lentils, and red chile peppers. Cook until the mustard seeds start to splutter, about 1 minute. Add the onion and green chile peppers and cook until the onion starts to brown around the edges, 3 to 4 minutes.

2. Stir in the kale and salt, cover, and cook until the greens are tender, 6 to 8 minutes. Add the grated coconut, mix well, and cook for 2 minutes. Serve hot or warm.

Panch Misali Charchari (Bengali Vegetable Curry)

PREP TIME: 10 minutes   COOK TIME: 20 minutes   TOTAL TIME: 30 minutes

This Bengali mixed vegetable dish is traditionally made with five ("panch" in Hindi/Bengali) different vegetables. The specific veggies are chosen to complement each other both in terms of texture and flavor, but feel free to use what you have in the refrigerator. Carrot, radish, and cabbage are good to use in this recipe, for example. Serve with Basmati Rice (page 121) or plain Paratha (page 112) for a filling meal. SERVES 6

2 tablespoons vegetable or canola oil, or Ghee (page 167)

2 teaspoons Panch Phoron (page 171)

1 bay leaf

2 dried red chile peppers, broken

2 green chile peppers, sliced

1 cup cauliflower florets

1 cup cubed pumpkin or butternut squash

2 or 3 baby eggplants, chopped

1 cup chopped green beans (1-inch pieces)

1 small zucchini, diced

1 cup water

½ cup green peas

¼ teaspoon ground turmeric

¼ teaspoon sugar

1 teaspoon salt

1. Heat the oil in a large skillet over medium heat. Add the panch phoron, bay leaf, and red chile peppers, and cook for 1 minute or until fragrant. Stir in the green chile peppers, cauliflower, pumpkin, eggplant, green beans, zucchini, and water. Mix well. Cover and cook until the veggies are tender, 10 to 12 minutes.

2. Stir in the green peas, turmeric, sugar, and salt. Cook for 2 to 3 minutes for all the flavors to mingle. Serve hot.

Pumpkin in Mustard Sauce

PREP TIME: 10 minutes, plus 30 minutes to rest
COOK TIME: 20 minutes   **TOTAL TIME:** 1 hour

Mustard oil and ground mustard are used widely in quite a few Indian cuisines, such as Bengali, Himachal Pradesh, and Kashmiri. In this recipe, ground mustard seed paste is added to cooked pumpkin, giving a spicy, pungent flavor to this otherwise sweet squash. Dry mango powder (amchur) adds a slight tang that balances the sweet and bitter flavors. Serve with Basmati Rice (page 121) and Bengali Masoor Dal (page 93) for a filling meal. SERVES 4

2 teaspoons
   mustard seeds

1 teaspoon uncooked rice

3 tablespoons water

1 tablespoon vegetable or
   canola oil

1 bay leaf

2 teaspoons Panch Phoron
   (page 171)

2 dried red chile
   peppers, broken

1 small pumpkin, peeled
   and diced (4 to 5 cups)

¼ teaspoon ground
   turmeric

1 teaspoon ground
   coriander seeds

1 teaspoon dry mango
   powder (amchur)

1 teaspoon salt

1. In a small bowl, combine the mustard seeds, rice, and water. Let rest for 30 minutes. Blend to a smooth paste and set aside.

2. Heat the oil in a skillet over medium heat. Add the bay leaf, panch phoron, and red chile peppers, and cook for 1 minute or until the spices are toasted and fragrant. Add the pumpkin and toss well to coat with the spices and oil. Cover and cook until the pumpkin is tender, stirring occasionally, about 12 to 15 minutes.

3. Stir in the turmeric, coriander, mango powder, and salt. Cook for 1 to 2 minutes. Add the mustard paste, cook for 2 more minutes, and turn off the heat. Serve hot.

Tip: Although in India this dish is traditionally made with pumpkin, you can substitute any winter squash, such as butternut, acorn, or delicata.

Kohlrabi Curry

PREP TIME: 15 minutes   **COOK TIME:** 30 minutes   **TOTAL TIME:** 45 minutes

In my opinion, kohlrabi is an underused vegetable that has a lot of potential. I use it in stir-fries, as in this recipe, or to make Sambar (page 87) or add, grated, to Kachumber (Cucumber Salad, page 140). In the United States it is available all year long. It has a crisp texture with a mild, sweet taste. In this curry, kohlrabi is cooked in an onion-tomato mixture and goes great with Basmati Rice (page 121) or plain Paratha (page 112). **SERVES 4**

1 tablespoon vegetable or
   canola oil

½ teaspoon mustard seeds

½ teaspoon cumin seeds

1 medium onion, chopped

2 garlic cloves,
   finely minced

2 medium kohlrabi, peeled
   and diced

½ cup water

2 medium
   tomatoes, chopped

¾ teaspoon
   cayenne pepper

1 teaspoon sugar

2 teaspoons tamarind
   concentrate

1 teaspoon salt

1. Heat the oil in a skillet over medium heat. Add the mustard seeds and cumin seeds and, once the seeds start to splutter, add the onion and garlic and cook until the onion turns lightly browned around the edges, 4 to 5 minutes.

2. Add the kohlrabi and water and bring to a boil over medium-high heat. Lower the heat, cover the pan, and cook, stirring occasionally, until the kohlrabi is fork-tender, 12 to 15 minutes. Stir in the tomatoes, cayenne, sugar, tamarind, and salt. Cover and cook until the tomato is soft and slightly mushy. Taste and adjust the seasoning. Serve hot.

Tip: If you like a spicy curry, omit the tamarind and sugar.

Zucchini Dry Curry

PREP TIME: 10 minutes, plus 30 minutes to soak

COOK TIME: 15 minutes   TOTAL TIME: 55 minutes

Simple dry curries like this one are usually a part of everyday meals in most Indian households. These curries focus on highlighting the vegetable and use only a handful of ingredients. Soaked split skinned moong dal (mung beans) add protein to the dish. Green beans or cauliflower can be substituted for the zucchini, giving you lots of options. Serve with Basmati Rice (page 121), plain Paratha (page 112), and Raita (page 169) for a wholesome meal. SERVES 4

½ cup split skinned mung beans (moong dal)

1 tablespoon vegetable or canola oil

½ teaspoon mustard seeds

½ teaspoon cumin seeds

1 dried red chile pepper, broken

2 medium zucchini, diced

2 green chile peppers, sliced

3 tablespoons grated fresh or dried unsweetened coconut

1 teaspoon salt

1. Soak the lentils in 1 cup of water for at least 30 minutes. Drain and set aside.

2. Heat the oil in a large skillet over medium heat. Add the mustard seeds, cumin seeds, and red chile and, once the seeds start to splutter, add the zucchini, green chiles, and lentils. Mix well to coat the zucchini pieces with the oil mixture. Cover and cook, stirring occasionally, until the zucchini and lentils are tender but not mushy, 8 to 10 minutes.

3. Stir in the coconut and salt. Mix well and cook for another 2 minutes. Serve hot or at room temperature.

Sweet Potato Curry

PREP TIME: 10 minutes   COOK TIME: 15 minutes   TOTAL TIME: 25 minutes

This sweet potato stir-fry can be made in less than half an hour, start to finish. Flavored with homemade garam masala, it is mildly spiced, but if you want a bit more heat, stir in ½ teaspoon of cayenne pepper. The roasted peanuts add crunch and texture. Serve with Basmati Rice (page 121) and your favorite dal. SERVES 4

1 tablespoon vegetable or canola oil

½ teaspoon mustard seeds

½ teaspoon cumin seeds

2 dried red chile peppers, broken

2 medium sweet potatoes, peeled and diced into ½-inch cubes

6 curry leaves

¼ cup water

½ teaspoon Garam Masala (page 164)

2 tablespoons coarsely chopped roasted, unsalted peanuts

1 teaspoon salt

1. Heat the oil in a skillet over medium heat. Add the mustard seeds, cumin seeds, and red chiles, and cook for 30 to 45 seconds or until the seeds splutter. Add the sweet potato and curry leaves and cook for 2 to 3 minutes, stirring to coat the sweet potatoes with the oil. Stir in the water, cover, and simmer until the sweet potato is tender, 6 to 8 minutes.

2. Add the garam masala, roasted peanuts, and salt, and mix well. Cook for 2 to 3 more minutes. Serve hot.

Tips: If you only have roasted salted peanuts, reduce the amount of salt to ½ teaspoon. You can substitute carrot, pumpkin, or butternut squash for the sweet potato.

Malai Kofta page 100

5
Dals, Legumes, and Curries

Dal Makhani

PREP TIME: 10 minutes, plus 8 hours to soak   COOK TIME: 1 hour

TOTAL TIME: 9 hours, 10 minutes

Dal makhani *literally means "butter lentils" in Hindi. True to its name, this is a buttery and rich lentil preparation popular in Indian restaurants all over the world. In this recipe, whole black lentils are slow-cooked until they become very smooth and creamy. This is a great dish to make for dinner parties because it can be made ahead of time and it reheats beautifully. Serve it over Basmati Rice (page 121) or with any Indian bread.* SERVES 6

¾ cup whole dried black lentils (urad dal), sorted, rinsed, and drained

¼ cup dried red kidney beans, sorted, rinsed, and drained, or ½ cup canned beans, drained and rinsed

5 cups water, divided

1½ teaspoons salt, divided

1 tablespoon vegetable or canola oil

2 tablespoons Ghee (page 167) **or unsalted butter, divided**

1 medium onion, finely chopped

2 green chile peppers, finely chopped

1½ teaspoons Ginger-Garlic Paste (page 172)

1 cup tomato puree

¼ teaspoon ground turmeric

1. In a medium bowl, combine the lentils, kidney beans, and enough water to cover them by 2 inches. Soak for at least 8 hours or overnight.

2. When you're ready to cook, drain the water from the lentils and kidney beans and put them in a medium saucepan over medium-high heat with 4 cups of water and ½ teaspoon of salt. Bring to a boil. Lower the heat, cover the pan, and simmer until the lentils and beans are tender, 40 to 45 minutes. Stir occasionally and add more water if needed.

3. While the lentils and beans are cooking, heat the oil and 1 tablespoon of ghee in a medium skillet over medium heat. Add the onion, chile peppers, and ginger-garlic paste, and cook until the onion is lightly browned around the edges, 4 to 5 minutes.

4. Stir in the tomato puree, turmeric, cayenne, coriander, cumin, and remaining 1 teaspoon of salt and cook, covered, until the oil starts to separate around the edges, 6 to 8 minutes. Add the tomato mixture to the lentils, mix well, and cook, covered, for 12 to 15 minutes.

1 teaspoon cayenne pepper

1½ teaspoons ground coriander

1 teaspoon ground cumin

¼ cup heavy cream

½ teaspoon Garam Masala (page 164)

2 tablespoons finely chopped fresh cilantro

5. Stir in the cream and garam masala and cook until heated through, 2 to 3 minutes. Turn off the heat, add the remaining 1 tablespoon of ghee, and sprinkle in the cilantro. Mix well to combine and serve hot.

Tip: If making ahead of time, make the recipe through step 4 and let it cool completely. Store in an airtight container in the refrigerator for up to 3 days or in the freezer for up to 1 month. To serve, reheat until simmering, then continue with step 5. Do not refreeze the dish.

Chana Masala

PREP TIME: 10 minutes   COOK TIME: 30 minutes   TOTAL TIME: 40 minutes

This is one of the most popular North Indian dishes both in restaurants and on street corners in India. Cooked chickpeas have a pleasant creamy texture that absorbs the spices and makes this curry tangy and spicy. Traditionally, chana masala is served with Bhatura (page 116) or Poori (page 120), but it can also be served over Samosas (page 12). SERVES 6

2 (15.5-ounce) cans chickpeas (or 1 cup dried, soaked, and cooked; see page 7)

2 tablespoons canola oil

1 teaspoon cumin seeds

1 medium onion, finely chopped

2 green chile peppers, halved lengthwise

1 teaspoon Ginger-Garlic Paste (page 172)

1 cup tomato puree

¼ teaspoon ground turmeric

½ teaspoon ground cumin

½ teaspoon ground coriander

½ teaspoon cayenne pepper

1 teaspoon Chole Masala (page 175)

¾ teaspoon dried mango powder (amchur powder)

1 teaspoon salt

1 cup water

2 tablespoons finely chopped fresh cilantro

1. Rinse and drain the canned chickpeas. Remove ½ cup of chickpeas and blend them to a smooth paste, adding a little water. Set aside.

2. Heat the oil in a medium saucepan over medium heat. Add the cumin seeds and cook for 30 seconds. Add the onion, green chile peppers, and ginger-garlic paste and cook, stirring frequently, until the onion is lightly browned around the edges, 3 to 4 minutes.

3. Stir in the tomato puree, turmeric, ground cumin, coriander, cayenne, chole masala, dried mango powder, and salt. Cook, covered, for 6 to 8 minutes, stirring occasionally.

4. Add the whole and blended chickpeas along with the water. Simmer for 8 to 10 minutes, adding more water if needed. Chana masala will thicken as it cools. Sprinkle with the cilantro and serve warm.

Rajma Masala

PREP TIME: 20 minutes   COOK TIME: 30 minutes   TOTAL TIME: 50 minutes

This hearty and comforting dish is an Indian version of chili. Kidney beans are a staple in Punjab, a North Indian state, and these earthy beans feature in many dishes from this region. The caramelized onion paste in the sauce adds a nice depth of flavor. Traditionally, rajma is served with Basmati Rice (page 121) for a satisfying and wholesome meal, but it can also be served with Naan (page 108) or Paratha (page 112). SERVES 6

3 tablespoons vegetable or canola oil, divided

1 medium onion, chopped

1 teaspoon Ginger-Garlic Paste (page 172)

1 cup tomato puree

¼ teaspoon ground turmeric

¾ teaspoon cayenne pepper

1 teaspoon ground coriander

1 teaspoon salt

1 cup water

2 (15.5-ounce) cans red kidney beans, rinsed and drained (or 1 cup dried, soaked and cooked; see page 7)

¾ teaspoon Garam Masala (page 164)

2 teaspoons crushed dried fenugreek leaves (kasoori methi)

2 tablespoons finely chopped fresh cilantro

1. Heat 1 tablespoon of oil in a large skillet over medium heat. Add the onion and cook, stirring occasionally, until lightly browned, 6 to 8 minutes. Stir in the ginger-garlic paste and cook for 1 minute. Transfer the mixture to a bowl, let it cool, and then grind it to a smooth paste, adding a little water if needed.

2. Heat the remaining 2 tablespoons of oil in the same skillet over medium heat. Add the tomato puree, turmeric, cayenne, coriander, and salt, and mix well. Cover and simmer for 5 to 7 minutes or until the oil starts to separate around the edges.

3. Stir in the onion paste and water and cook for 3 to 4 minutes. The mixture will splatter a little bit at this stage, so stay back and keep the lid handy to cover the skillet. Add more water if the mixture looks too thick. Please note that the sauce will thicken as it cools, so adjust the consistency accordingly.

4. Stir in the beans and simmer for 12 to 15 minutes. Add the garam masala and fenugreek and cook for 2 more minutes. Stir in the cilantro. Serve hot.

Dal Tadka

PREP TIME: 10 minutes   COOK TIME: 45 minutes   TOTAL TIME: 55 minutes

This is a simple lentil dish elevated by the addition of tempering (tadka) just before serving. The spiced ghee adds tons of flavor and aroma to the dal. This is my favorite dish to make for large groups because it is easy to prepare and is always a hit with my friends and family. Serve with Basmati Rice (page 121) or with your favorite Indian bread. **SERVES 6**

½ cup dried split skinned pigeon peas (toor dal), rinsed and drained

¼ cup dried yellow split peas (chana dal), rinsed and drained

3 cups water

1 tablespoon vegetable or canola oil

1 medium onion, finely chopped

2 teaspoons peeled grated fresh ginger

2 garlic cloves, finely minced

1 medium tomato, chopped

¼ teaspoon ground turmeric

½ teaspoon cayenne pepper

1 teaspoon ground coriander

1¼ teaspoons salt

2 tablespoons finely chopped fresh cilantro

1 tablespoon Ghee
(page 167)

1 teaspoon cumin seeds

2 dried red chile peppers, broken

⅛ teaspoon asafetida

1. Combine the pigeon peas, yellow split peas, and water in a medium saucepan over medium-high heat. Bring to a boil. Reduce the heat to medium-low, cover the pan, and simmer, stirring occasionally, until the peas are tender, 25 to 30 minutes.

2. While the dals are cooking, heat the oil in a medium skillet over medium heat. Add the onion, ginger, and garlic, and cook until the onion is lightly browned around the edges. Stir in the tomato, turmeric, cayenne, coriander, and salt. Cook until the tomatoes are mushy, 3 to 4 minutes.

3. Stir the tomato mixture into the cooked lentils along with ½ to 1 cup of water. Simmer for 6 to 8 minutes. Turn off the heat and add the cilantro.

4. Heat the ghee in a small saucepan over medium heat. Add the cumin seeds and dried red chiles and cook for 1 minute. Stir in the asafetida and add the tadka to the lentils. Mix well and serve hot.

Black-Eyed Pea Curry

PREP TIME: 15 minutes   COOK TIME: 25 minutes   TOTAL TIME: 40 minutes

Black-eyed peas have a wonderfully creamy texture and earthy, nutty taste. I always have some dried black-eyed peas on hand since they are very easy to cook from dried. But canned beans are equally delicious and convenient, and are what I use here to make this dish a quick and easy one. Mushrooms accentuate the earthiness of this curry. Serve with Basmati Rice (page 121) or any Indian bread. SERVES 6

1 tablespoon vegetable or canola oil

1 medium onion, finely chopped

1 teaspoon Ginger-Garlic Paste (page 172)

1 cup mushrooms, chopped

1 medium carrot, peeled and diced

1 cup tomato puree

1 (15.5-ounce) can black-eyed peas, rinsed and drained

¼ teaspoon ground turmeric

½ teaspoon cayenne pepper

½ teaspoon ground cumin

1 teaspoon salt

½ cup water

½ cup coconut milk, preferably full-fat

½ teaspoon Garam Masala (page 164)

2 tablespoons finely chopped fresh cilantro

1. Heat the oil in a large skillet over medium heat. Add the onion and ginger-garlic paste and cook until the onion is lightly browned around the edges, 3 to 4 minutes. Add the mushrooms and carrot, cover, and cook until the veggies are tender, 5 to 6 minutes.

2. Stir in the tomato puree, black-eyed peas, turmeric, cayenne, cumin, salt, and water, and simmer for 8 to 10 minutes. Add the coconut milk and garam masala and cook until heated through, 2 to 3 minutes. Stir in the cilantro and serve hot.

Tip: To cook dried black-eyed peas, soak them overnight in lots of water. Rinse and drain the beans, then combine them with 3 cups of water in a medium saucepan and bring to a boil over medium-high heat. Lower the heat, cover, and cook until the beans are tender, 40 to 45 minutes. Drain the beans and reserve their cooking water to add instead of water in the recipe.

Chana Saag

PREP TIME: 10 minutes   COOK TIME: 20 minutes   TOTAL TIME: 30 minutes

This is a very popular restaurant dish that is easy to make at home. Chana saag *means "chickpeas with greens" in Hindi. So, as you might have guessed, this recipe is a scrumptious combination of hearty beans and greens. My recipe is a lighter version of the traditional recipe because it uses much less oil and is mildly spiced. Serve with Basmati Rice (page 121) or your favorite Indian bread.* SERVES 4

- 2 tablespoons vegetable or canola oil
- 1 medium onion, finely chopped
- 1 teaspoon Ginger-Garlic Paste (page 172)
- 2 medium tomatoes, chopped
- ¼ teaspoon ground turmeric
- ¾ teaspoon cayenne pepper
- 1 teaspoon ground coriander
- 1 teaspoon salt
- 1 pound fresh spinach, chopped, or 1 (10-ounce) box chopped frozen spinach, thawed
- 1½ cups cooked chickpeas or 1 (15-ounce) can chickpeas, rinsed and drained
- 1 cup water
- 1 tablespoon freshly squeezed lemon juice

1. Heat the oil in a large skillet over medium heat. Add the onion and ginger-garlic paste and cook until the onion is lightly browned around the edges, 3 to 4 minutes. Stir in the tomatoes, turmeric, cayenne, coriander, and salt. Mix well, cover, and cook for 3 to 4 minutes or until the tomatoes are soft and mushy.

2. Add the chopped spinach in batches, if needed, and cook until the leaves are wilted and tender, 4 to 5 minutes. Add the chickpeas and water and simmer the mixture for 5 minutes. Stir in the lemon juice, mix well, and serve hot.

Tip: This is a versatile dish that can be made with any green leafy vegetable such as kale, mustard greens, or Swiss chard. If using hearty greens, cook them a little longer, 8 to 10 minutes, before adding the beans. Black-eyed peas or any small white beans, such as cannellini or navy beans, can be substituted for the chickpeas.

Sambar

PREP TIME: 20 minutes   COOK TIME: 40 minutes   TOTAL TIME: 1 hour

Sambar is a quintessential South Indian lentil and vegetable stew. It is often part of an everyday meal served with plain rice for lunch or as an accompaniment to Dosa (page 118) or Upma (page 129) for breakfast. Homemade Sambar Masala (page 176) adds a beautiful aroma and flavor to this dish. Leftovers are great the next day because the broth and veggies have an opportunity to absorb all the flavors. Reheat before serving. SERVES 6

½ cup dried split skinned pigeon peas (toor dal), rinsed and drained

4 cups water, divided

1 small red onion, chopped

1 small carrot, peeled and chopped

4 small red radishes, quartered

1 small green bell pepper, cubed

1 tablespoon tamarind concentrate

1½ tablespoons Sambar Masala (page 176)

1¼ teaspoons salt

2 green chile peppers, sliced

1 tablespoon vegetable or canola oil

1 teaspoon mustard seeds

⅛ teaspoon asafetida (hing)

8 curry leaves

2 tablespoons finely chopped fresh cilantro

1. Combine the pigeon peas and 2½ cups of water in a medium saucepan and bring to a boil over high heat. Lower the heat and simmer, covered, stirring occasionally, until the peas are tender, 20 to 25 minutes.

2. While the peas are cooking, in a medium saucepan over medium-high heat, combine the onion, carrot, radishes, bell pepper, tamarind, sambar masala, salt, and the remaining 1½ cups of water. Bring to a boil, lower the heat, and simmer uncovered until the veggies are fork-tender, 12 to 15 minutes.

3. Add the cooked lentils and the remaining cooking water to the veggie mixture. Mix well and simmer for 10 minutes.

4. In a small skillet, heat the oil over medium heat. Add the mustard seeds and, once they start to splutter, add the asafetida and curry leaves, and cook for 30 seconds. Pour this hot oil into the lentil mixture. Mix well. Turn off the heat and stir in the cilantro. Serve hot.

Rasam

PREP TIME: 10 minutes **COOK TIME:** 45 minutes **TOTAL TIME:** 55 minutes

This spicy, broth-like soup was originally known as "mulliga thanni" in South India. This literally translates to "pepper water," indicating the spiciness of the dish. A freshly ground spice powder made with peppercorns and coriander seeds adds a nice flavor to the rasam. The tang from tomatoes and tamarind concentrate balances out the spiciness beautifully. Serve with Basmati Rice (page 121) as part of a meal or as a light soup. SERVES 6

1 teaspoon
   coriander seeds

1 teaspoon cumin seeds

¼ teaspoon black
   peppercorns

3 tablespoons split pigeon
   peas (toor dal)

4 cups water, divided

2 medium
   tomatoes, chopped

1 teaspoon tamarind
   concentrate

⅛ teaspoon
   asafetida (hing)

1 teaspoon salt

2 teaspoons Ghee
   (page 167), **or vegetable
   or canola oil**

1 teaspoon mustard seeds

½ teaspoon cumin seeds

1 dried red chile
   pepper, broken

6 curry leaves

1. In a small skillet over medium heat, dry roast the coriander seeds, cumin seeds, and peppercorns, stirring frequently, until they are aromatic, 3 to 4 minutes. Remove the skillet from the heat and set the spices aside to cool. Once they are cool enough to handle, grind them to a powder in a spice grinder or with a mortar and pestle. Set aside.

2. In a medium saucepan over medium-high heat, combine the pigeon peas with 2 cups of water and bring to a boil. Lower the heat to medium, cover, and simmer until the peas are very tender, 20 to 25 minutes.

3. Transfer the cooked peas and the cooking liquid to a blender and blend to a smooth mixture. Or, you could use an immersion blender right in the saucepan.

4. Return the peas to the saucepan. Add the tomatoes, tamarind, spice powder from step 1, asafetida, salt, and the remaining 2 cups of water. Bring to a boil over high heat, lower the heat, and simmer for 10 minutes.

5. Heat the ghee in a small skillet over medium heat. Add the mustard seeds, cumin seeds, and red chile and, once the seeds start to splutter, add the curry leaves. Pour the hot ghee into the tomato-lentil mixture, stir well, and serve hot.

Palak Dal

PREP TIME: 10 minutes   COOK TIME: 45 minutes   TOTAL TIME: 55 minutes

The combination of lentils with leafy greens is nutritious and delicious at the same time. This dal is a family favorite that I make at least once a week. Frozen spinach is a staple in my home, and it makes cooking this dish easy and convenient, even on a weeknight. Swiss chard or kale can be substituted for the spinach. If using kale, cook for 8 to 10 minutes, until the leaves are tender. Serve with Basmati Rice (page 121) and a stir-fry. SERVES 4

1 tablespoon vegetable or
    canola oil

½ teaspoon mustard seeds

½ teaspoon cumin seeds

1 garlic clove,
    finely minced

1 teaspoon peeled grated
    fresh ginger

1 small onion, chopped

1 medium tomato, chopped

¼ teaspoon
    cayenne pepper

½ teaspoon Garam Masala
    (page 164)

½ cup dried split pigeon
    peas (toor dal), rinsed
    and drained

2½ cups water

3 cups fresh spinach
    leaves, coarsely
    chopped, or 1 cup frozen
    chopped spinach

1 teaspoon salt

1. Heat the oil in a medium saucepan over medium heat. Add the mustard seeds and cumin seeds and, once the seeds start to splutter, add the garlic, ginger, and onion. Cook until the onion is translucent, 2 to 3 minutes.

2. Add the tomato, cayenne, and garam masala. Mix well and cook for 2 minutes.

3. Stir in the pigeon peas and water and bring to a boil over medium-high heat. Reduce the heat to low, cover partially, and simmer until the lentils are tender, about 30 minutes. Add more water if you want the dal to be thinner.

4. Add the spinach and salt, cover, and simmer until the spinach is wilted and cooked, 3 to 4 minutes. Serve hot.

Panchmel Dal (Five-Lentil Stew)

PREP TIME: 10 minutes   **COOK TIME:** 45 minutes   **TOTAL TIME:** 55 minutes

This hearty stew is made with five kinds of lentils, each one of which adds a different flavor and texture to the dish. Using split skinned lentils expedites the cooking process, but whole lentils can also be used, in which case they need to be soaked first for at least 4 hours. Proceed as written in the recipe and cook for 40 minutes or until tender. SERVES 6

2 tablespoons dried split pigeon peas (toor dal)

2 tablespoons dried split mung beans (moong dal)

2 tablespoons dried red lentils (masoor dal)

2 tablespoons dried yellow split peas (chana dal)

2 tablespoons dried split black lentils (urad dal)

4 cups water, divided

2 tablespoons Ghee (page 167), **or vegetable or canola oil**

1 teaspoon cumin seeds

⅛ teaspoon asafetida

2 dried red chile peppers, broken

2 teaspoons peeled grated fresh ginger

1 large onion, chopped

2 green chile peppers, sliced

1 medium tomato, chopped

¼ teaspoon ground turmeric

1 teaspoon Garam Masala (page 164)

1 teaspoon salt

2 tablespoons finely chopped fresh cilantro

1. Combine the lentils and rinse and drain them well. Put them in a medium saucepan over medium-high heat with 3 cups of water. Bring to a boil. Lower the heat and simmer until the lentils are tender, 20 to 25 minutes. Add more water if the mixture looks too thick.

2. Heat the oil in a medium skillet over medium heat. Add the cumin seeds and cook for 30 seconds, then add the asafetida, red chiles, and ginger, and cook for 1 minute or until fragrant. Add the onion and green chiles and cook until the onion is lightly browned around the edges, 3 to 4 minutes. Stir in the tomato and turmeric and cook until the tomato turns tender and mushy, 3 to 4 minutes.

3. Add the tomato mixture to the dal mixture along with the remaining 1 cup of water, the garam masala, and the salt. Simmer for 8 to 10 minutes for the flavors to combine. Sprinkle with the cilantro and serve hot.

Tomato Moong Dal

PREP TIME: 10 minutes   **COOK TIME:** 30 minutes   **TOTAL TIME:** 40 minutes

This is one of my favorite dishes from childhood. My mom used to make this easy, comforting stew at least once a week for us. Now I make it for my kids, and I am glad that they enjoy it as much as I did. This is a simple dal that is great to serve hot with Basmati Rice (page 121) and a generous dollop of homemade Ghee (page 167). SERVES 6

½ cup split skinned mung beans (moong dal)

2 medium ripe tomatoes, chopped

2 green chile peppers, sliced

2 cups water

¼ teaspoon ground turmeric

½ teaspoon cayenne pepper

1 teaspoon salt

2 teaspoons vegetable or canola oil

1 teaspoon mustard seeds

1 teaspoon cumin seeds

1 dried red chile pepper

⅛ teaspoon asafetida (hing)

2 tablespoons freshly squeezed lemon juice

1. In a medium saucepan over medium-high heat, combine the mung beans, tomatoes, green chiles, and water. Bring to a boil. Lower the heat, cover the pan, and cook until the mung beans are tender and turning mushy, 20 to 25 minutes.

2. Stir in the turmeric, cayenne, and salt, and simmer for 5 more minutes. Turn off the heat.

3. Heat the oil in a small skillet over medium heat. Add the mustard seeds and cumin seeds and cook until they start to splutter. Add the dried red chile and asafetida and cook for 30 seconds. Turn off the heat and add the hot oil to the cooked mung beans. Stir in the lemon juice and mix well to combine. Serve hot.

Bengali Masoor Dal

PREP TIME: 10 minutes   **COOK TIME:** 30 minutes   **TOTAL TIME:** 40 minutes

This dal is made with simple ingredients but is packed with flavor from the addition of panch phoron, or Bengali five-spice blend. Tempering (tadka) made with this spice blend elevates a humble everyday dish to something that is rich and aromatic. When cooked in hot oil, the spices pop and release a beautiful aroma and add their characteristic taste to this dal. Serve with any Indian bread or Basmati Rice (page 121). **SERVES 4**

½ cup dried red lentils
   (masoor dal)

2 cups water

¼ teaspoon ground
   turmeric

1 teaspoon vegetable or
   canola oil

1 teaspoon Panch Phoron
   (page 171)

1 small red onion,
   finely chopped

2 green chile
   peppers, sliced

2 medium tomatoes,
   finely chopped

1 teaspoon salt

2 tablespoons freshly
   squeezed lemon juice

2 tablespoons finely
   chopped fresh cilantro

1. In a medium saucepan over medium-high heat, combine the lentils, water, and turmeric. Bring to a boil. Lower the heat, cover the pan, and simmer until the lentils are tender, 15 to 20 minutes.

2. While the lentils are cooking, heat the oil in a small skillet over medium heat. Add the panch phoron and cook for 1 minute or until fragrant. Add the onion and chiles and cook until the onion turns translucent, 2 to 3 minutes. Stir in the tomatoes and salt and cook until the tomatoes are soft and mushy, 3 to 4 minutes.

3. Add the tomato mixture to the lentils. If the dal looks too thick, add ¼ to ½ cup of water and simmer for 4 to 5 minutes. Turn off the heat and add the lemon juice and cilantro. Mix well and serve hot.

Tip: If you do not have panch phoron on hand, use ¼ teaspoon each of mustard seeds and cumin seeds. Add 2 finely minced garlic cloves along with the onion to add flavor to the dal.

Gatte ki Subzi (Chickpea Flour Dumpling Curry)

PREP TIME: 20 minutes   COOK TIME: 35 minutes   TOTAL TIME: 55 minutes

This is a traditional dish from the desert state of Rajasthan. As it is an arid region with sparse vegetation, the local cuisine relies heavily on lentils, dairy, and dried or preserved foods such as Masala Papad (page 21). Chickpea flour is a staple ingredient because chickpeas grow plentifully in the region. In this dish, chickpea flour is used to make dumplings that are then simmered in a simple yogurt sauce. Serve with Methi Roti (page 110) for a delicious Rajasthani meal. SERVES 4

1 cup chickpea flour (besan)

½ teaspoon ground cumin

1 teaspoon ground coriander

1 teaspoon cayenne pepper, divided

1¼ teaspoons salt, divided

2 tablespoons vegetable or canola oil, divided

3 cups water

½ teaspoon cumin seeds

1 medium onion, finely chopped

1 teaspoon Ginger-Garlic Paste (page 172)

¼ teaspoon turmeric

1 teaspoon Garam Masala (page 164)

1 cup Yogurt (page 168), whisked

2 tablespoons finely chopped fresh cilantro

1. In a medium bowl, sift the chickpea flour to make sure there are no lumps. Add the cumin, coriander, ½ teaspoon of cayenne, ½ teaspoon of salt, and 1 tablespoon of oil, and mix well. Add 2 to 3 tablespoons of water, 1 tablespoon at a time, while mixing with a spoon until a sticky dough forms. Lightly grease your hands and knead the dough. Divide the dough into 6 equal portions and roll each portion into a 4-inch-long, ½-inch-wide log. Place the logs on a plate.

2. In a medium saucepan on high heat, bring the remaining water to a rolling boil. Lower the heat to medium and gently add the chickpea logs to the pan. Simmer for 15 to 20 minutes, stirring occasionally, until the logs are cooked through. (A sharp knife inserted into the center of the log should come out clean.) Using a slotted spoon, transfer the cooked gatte to a chopping board. Reserve the cooking water.

3. Once the gatte have cooled slightly, cut them into bite-size pieces, ½ inch long. Set aside.

4. Heat the remaining 1 tablespoon of oil in the same saucepan over medium heat. Add the cumin seeds and cook for 30 seconds. Add the onion and ginger-garlic paste and cook until the onion is translucent, 3 to 4 minutes. Stir in the turmeric, remaining ½ teaspoon of cayenne, garam masala, and remaining ¾ teaspoon of salt. Mix well and cook for 1 minute.

5. Lower the heat to medium-low and add the yogurt, stirring continuously until the spices are well incorporated. Add the reserved gatte cooking water and bring the mixture to a simmer. Add the gatte to the yogurt mixture and cook for 6 to 8 minutes. Turn off the heat and add the cilantro. Serve hot.

Tip: To make gatte ahead of time, make the recipe through step 3 and let them cool completely. Place them in a resealable freezer-safe bag and freeze for up to 2 months.

Dum Aloo

PREP TIME: 20 minutes   COOK TIME: 30 minutes   TOTAL TIME: 50 minutes

Dum aloo is a popular dish in India and has quite a few variations depending on the region. But in all versions, fried baby potatoes are simmered in a flavorful sauce. This version is from Lucknow in Uttar Pradesh and uses dry grated unsweetened coconut, cashews, and spices in the sauce. Milk is added to the sauce to balance the spiciness. Serve with your favorite Indian bread. SERVES 6

2 dried red chile peppers

1 tablespoon
   coriander seeds

2 teaspoons cumin seeds

1 (½-inch) piece
   cinnamon stick

2 whole cloves

4 black peppercorns

2 tablespoons
   unsweetened dried
   grated coconut

2 teaspoons white poppy
   seeds or cashews

¼ cup water

10 to 12 baby potatoes

2 tablespoons vegetable or
   canola oil, plus more for
   deep-frying

1 medium onion, grated

1 teaspoon Ginger-Garlic
   Paste (page 172)

1 teaspoon salt

1 cup tomato puree

½ cup whole milk

2 tablespoons finely
   chopped fresh cilantro

1. In a blender, combine the dried red chiles, coriander, cumin, cinnamon, cloves, peppercorns, coconut, poppy seeds, and water. Blend to make a smooth paste. Set aside.

2. Peel the potatoes and place them in a heavy-bottomed saucepan. Cover them with water and bring it to a boil over medium-high heat. Lower the heat and simmer until the potatoes are fork-tender, 10 to 12 minutes. Drain well and cool slightly. Using a fork, poke the boiled potatoes 2 or 3 times each.

3. Fill a medium wok or Dutch oven 2 inches deep with oil and heat it over medium-high heat to 350°F. Add the potatoes and fry until they are evenly golden on all sides. Use a slotted spoon to transfer them to a paper towel–lined plate and set aside.

4. Heat the remaining 2 tablespoons of oil in a medium skillet over medium heat. Add the onion and ginger-garlic paste and cook until the onion is lightly browned and does not smell raw anymore, 5 to 7 minutes.

5. Stir in the spice paste and salt and cook for 1 to 2 minutes for the spices to cook. Add the tomato puree and simmer for 4 to 5 minutes. Next, add the fried potatoes and ½ cup of water. Cover and simmer for 5 to 7 minutes for the flavors to mingle. Stir in the milk and cook until heated through, 2 to 3 minutes. Turn off the heat and add the cilantro. Serve hot.

Tip: To make this vegan, substitute unsweetened almond milk or oat milk for the dairy milk.

Mushroom Masala

PREP TIME: 10 minutes, plus 30 minutes to soak
COOK TIME: 20 minutes   **TOTAL TIME:** 1 hour

This mushroom masala is sure to please meat-eaters and vegetarians alike. Mushrooms are earthy, hearty, and combine deliciously with the spices used in the dish. This is a vegan curry that uses ground cashews or almonds to make the creamy, rich sauce. Serve with Basmati Rice (page 121) or any Indian bread. **SERVES 4**

2 tablespoons chopped cashews or almonds

8 ounces brown or white mushrooms (10 to 12 medium mushrooms)

2 tablespoons vegetable or canola oil

½ teaspoon cumin seeds

1 medium onion, finely chopped

1 teaspoon Ginger-Garlic Paste (page 172)

2 teaspoons tomato paste

½ cup tomato puree

¼ teaspoon ground turmeric

½ teaspoon cayenne pepper

½ teaspoon ground coriander

½ teaspoon ground cumin

1 teaspoon salt

½ teaspoon Garam Masala (page 164)

2 tablespoons finely chopped fresh cilantro

1. Soak the cashews in warm water for at least 30 minutes. Drain the cashews and grind them to a smooth paste in a blender or food processor.

2. Wipe the mushrooms thoroughly with a damp kitchen towel. Chop them into quarters or eighths depending on their size. Set aside.

3. Heat the oil in a medium skillet over medium heat. Add the cumin seeds and cook for 30 seconds. Add the onion and ginger-garlic paste and cook for 3 to 4 minutes, or until the onion starts to brown around the edges. Add the mushrooms and cook until they are tender, 5 to 7 minutes.

4. Stir in the tomato paste and cook for 1 to 2 minutes. Add the tomato puree, turmeric, cayenne, coriander, cumin, salt, and ½ cup of water. Bring the mixture to a simmer and cook for 4 to 5 minutes for the flavors to meld.

5. Add the cashew paste and garam masala and cook until heated through. Add ¼ cup of water if the mixture looks too dry, and bring the mixture back to a simmer. Turn off the heat and stir in the cilantro. Serve hot.

Vegetable Korma

PREP TIME: 20 minutes   **COOK TIME:** 25 minutes   **TOTAL TIME:** 45 minutes

Korma is a spicy curry made with a freshly ground spice paste. Grated coconut and cashews add richness and creaminess while yogurt adds tang and balances the other flavors beautifully. This version uses mixed vegetables, but the curry can be made with just potatoes or Paneer (page 170). Serve with Poori (page 120) or Dosa (page 118). **SERVES 4**

2 green chile peppers, chopped

2 garlic cloves

2 teaspoons peeled grated fresh ginger

½ cup grated coconut

10 cashews

1 teaspoon coriander seeds

¼ cup chopped fresh cilantro

¾ to 1 cup water, divided

2 tablespoons vegetable or canola oil

1 bay leaf

1 small onion, finely chopped

2 medium potatoes, peeled and diced

1 medium carrot, diced

½ cup chopped green beans, fresh or frozen

1 medium tomato, finely chopped

½ cup green peas

1 teaspoon Garam Masala (page 164)

1 teaspoon salt

½ cup Yogurt (page 168)

1. In a blender, combine the green chiles, garlic, ginger, coconut, cashews, coriander, cilantro, and ¼ cup of water and blend to a smooth paste. Add more water if the mixture looks too thick. Set aside until ready to use.

2. Heat the oil in a medium skillet over medium heat. Add the bay leaf and cook for 30 seconds. Add the onion and cook until translucent, 3 minutes. Add the potatoes, carrot, green beans, and ½ cup of water, cover, and cook until the veggies are tender, 8 to 10 minutes.

3. Add the tomato and cook until it turns soft and mushy. Stir in the peas, chile-garlic paste, garam masala, salt, and more water if the curry looks too thick. Mix well and simmer for 5 to 6 minutes for the flavors to come together.

4. Lower the heat and stir in the yogurt. Cook for 2 to 3 minutes or until heated through. Serve hot.

Tip: Frozen mixed vegetables come in very handy when making this dish. There is no need to thaw them; simply add them to the curry after the potatoes are cooked in step 2 and cook until the veggies are heated through.

Malai Kofta

PREP TIME: 15 minutes   COOK TIME: 45 minutes   TOTAL TIME: 1 hour

Malai kofta is a rich and decadent dish that is usually made for weddings or other special occasions. Croquettes made with potato and Paneer (page 170) are served with a creamy tomato sauce. The croquettes are crispy on the outside and soft on the inside. For the best texture, pour the sauce over the kofta just before serving. Serve with any Indian bread or Vegetable Biryani (page 124). SERVES 4

3 tablespoons vegetable or canola oil, divided, plus more for deep-frying

1 medium onion, chopped

1 teaspoon Ginger-Garlic Paste (page 172)

2 medium tomatoes, chopped

2 tablespoons chopped cashews, plus 4 cashews, chopped

1 tablespoon butter

1 bay leaf

¼ teaspoon ground turmeric

1 teaspoon chili powder

½ teaspoon ground coriander

½ teaspoon ground cumin

1½ teaspoons salt, divided

½ teaspoon Garam Masala (page 164)

1 teaspoon crushed dried fenugreek leaves (kasoori methi)

¾ cup water

1. Heat 1 tablespoon of oil in a large skillet over medium heat. Add the onion and cook until it turns lightly browned around the edges, 4 to 5 minutes. Stir in the ginger-garlic paste and cook for 1 minute. Add the tomatoes and 2 tablespoons of cashews and cook until the tomatoes turn mushy, 4 to 5 minutes. Turn off the heat and let it cool. Once the mixture is cool enough to handle, blend it to a smooth paste using an immersion blender (or in a countertop blender).

2. Heat the remaining 2 tablespoons of oil and the butter in a large skillet over medium heat. Add the bay leaf and cook for 30 seconds. Add the onion-tomato paste, turmeric, chili powder, coriander, cumin, and 1 teaspoon of salt, cover, and simmer for 7 to 8 minutes.

3. Add the garam masala, fenugreek, and water, and cook for 4 to 5 minutes or until simmering. Stir in the cream and cook until heated through. Remove and discard the bay leaf. Sprinkle the cream mixture with 2 tablespoons of cilantro and set aside.

- 3 tablespoons heavy cream
- 4 tablespoons finely chopped fresh cilantro, divided, plus more for sprinkling
- 2 medium potatoes, peeled, boiled, and mashed
- 1 cup paneer, store-bought or homemade (page 170), grated
- 1 teaspoon cayenne pepper
- 2 teaspoons peeled grated fresh ginger
- 6 to 8 golden raisins
- 2 tablespoons all-purpose flour
- Oil, for deep-frying

4. In a medium bowl, combine the mashed potato, paneer, cayenne, ginger, remaining 2 tablespoons of cilantro, remaining 4 chopped cashews, raisins, flour, and the remaining ½ teaspoon of salt. Mix and knead all into a smooth dough. Divide the dough into 8 to 10 lime-size balls.

5. Fill a medium wok or heavy-bottomed skillet 2 inches deep with oil and heat it over medium-high heat to 350°F. Working in batches, gently slide the kofta into the hot oil and fry until they are golden brown all over. Use a slotted spoon to transfer them to a paper towel-lined plate. Repeat with the remaining kofta.

6. Place the kofta on a serving plate or bowl, top them with the tomato sauce, and sprinkle with cilantro. Serve warm.

Tip: The tomato sauce can be made up to 3 days ahead of time. Cool it completely and store in an airtight container in the refrigerator. Note that the sauce will thicken as it chills, so add some water and reheat it just before pouring it over the hot kofta.

Vegetable Jalfrezi

PREP TIME: 15 minutes   **COOK TIME:** 20 minutes   **TOTAL TIME:** 35 minutes

Jalfrezi is a popular dish that uses the Chinese stir-frying technique but with Indian flavors. It is a versatile dish that can be made with different vegetables or proteins. In this vegetarian version, the mix of vegetables makes it colorful and inviting. The key to success with this stir-fry is to keep the veggies crisp-tender and not overcook them. Serve with any Indian bread or with Basmati Rice (page 121). **SERVES 4**

2 tablespoons vegetable or canola oil

½ teaspoon cumin seeds

1 small red onion, sliced

1 teaspoon Ginger-Garlic Paste (page 172)

1 green chile pepper, sliced

1 medium carrot, peeled and cut into thin diagonal slices

1 cup cauliflower florets

1 cup chopped green beans, fresh or frozen

1 medium green or red bell pepper, chopped

½ cup water

½ cup green peas, fresh or frozen

½ cup corn kernels, fresh or frozen

¼ teaspoon ground turmeric

½ teaspoon cayenne pepper

1 teaspoon salt

½ cup tomato puree

½ teaspoon Garam Masala (page 164)

1 teaspoon dried fenugreek leaves (kasoori methi)

2 tablespoons finely chopped fresh cilantro

1. Heat the oil in a medium skillet over medium heat. Add the cumin seeds and cook for 30 seconds. Add the onion, ginger-garlic paste, and chile pepper, and cook until the onion is lightly browned around the edges, 4 to 5 minutes.

2. Add the carrot, cauliflower, green beans, bell pepper, and water, and mix well. Cook, covered, until the veggies are crisp-tender, 6 to 8 minutes. Stir in the peas, corn, turmeric, cayenne, and salt. Mix well and cook for 2 minutes.

3. Add the tomato puree and simmer for 3 to 4 minutes. Stir in the garam masala and fenugreek and cook for 3 to 4 minutes more. Turn off the heat and add the cilantro. Serve hot.

Methi Chaman

PREP TIME: 20 minutes   **COOK TIME:** 30 minutes   **TOTAL TIME:** 50 minutes

Methi chaman is a Kashmiri dish that is made with fresh fenugreek leaves, spinach, and Paneer (page 170). The slight bitterness in fenugreek adds a unique flavor, and this is emphasized with the addition of dried fenugreek leaves (kasoori methi). Although it is not traditional, this dish can be made with Swiss chard or kale for an equally delicious alternative. **SERVES 4**

2 tablespoons vegetable or canola oil, divided

1 large onion, chopped

3 green chile peppers, sliced

3 tablespoons cashews

2 teaspoons peeled grated fresh ginger

2 garlic cloves

¼ cup tomato puree

1 teaspoon ground coriander

½ teaspoon cayenne pepper

3 cups fresh fenugreek leaves (methi), chopped

3 cups baby spinach, chopped

1 cup paneer, store-bought or homemade (page 170), cut into ½-inch cubes

3 tablespoons heavy cream

2 tablespoons dried fenugreek leaves

1 teaspoon Garam Masala (page 164)

1 teaspoon salt

1. Heat 1 tablespoon of oil in a medium skillet over medium heat. Add the onion, green chiles, cashews, ginger, and garlic, and cook until the onion turns translucent, 4 to 5 minutes. Turn off the heat and let the mixture cool for 10 minutes. Blend the mixture to a smooth paste in a blender.

2. Heat the remaining 1 tablespoon of oil in the same skillet over medium heat. Add the onion paste and cook for 2 to 3 minutes. If it starts to splutter, cover the pan with a lid. Stir in the tomato puree, coriander, and cayenne, and cook for 5 to 6 minutes.

3. Add the fresh fenugreek and the spinach, cover, and cook until the leaves are wilted and do not smell raw anymore, 5 to 6 minutes. Add the paneer and mix gently to coat the pieces with the green sauce.

4. Stir in the cream, dried fenugreek, garam masala, and salt. Mix well and cook for 3 to 4 minutes for the flavors to come together. Serve hot.

Tip: Frozen greens can be used instead of fresh. Frozen fenugreek (methi) leaves are available in Indian grocery stores.

Mutter Paneer (Paneer and Pea Curry)

PREP TIME: 10 minutes   COOK TIME: 15 minutes   TOTAL TIME: 25 minutes

This is the first recipe I learned to make with paneer. It is one of the simplest recipes, and even a novice cook can master it in no time. I did not alter the original recipe much over the years and my kids devour it every time I make this curry. Paneer (page 170) is the star of this recipe, and the other ingredients complement it beautifully. Tomatoes and green peas add color and texture. Serve with Naan (page 108) or plain Paratha (page 112). SERVES 4

1 tablespoon vegetable or canola oil

1 teaspoon cumin seeds

1 medium red onion, finely chopped

2 teaspoons peeled grated fresh ginger

1 green chile pepper, sliced

1 medium tomato, finely chopped

½ teaspoon cayenne pepper

½ teaspoon Garam Masala (page 164)

¾ teaspoon salt

1 cup cubed Paneer (page 170) (½-inch cubes)

½ cup green peas, fresh or frozen

1 cup water

2 tablespoons finely chopped fresh cilantro

1. Heat the oil in a medium skillet over medium heat. Add the cumin seeds and cook for 30 seconds. Add the onion, ginger, and green chile, and cook until the onion is translucent, 3 to 4 minutes. Stir in the tomato, cayenne, garam masala, and salt. Cook for 2 to 3 minutes or until the tomatoes turn soft and mushy.

2. Add the paneer, green peas, and water, and bring the mixture to a boil. Lower the heat and simmer until the peas are tender and the sauce is thick, 8 to 10 minutes. Turn off the heat and stir in the cilantro. Serve hot.

Tip: To make this dish a little special, shallow-fry the paneer in a little oil until it's golden on all sides. Add the fried paneer cubes to the tomato mixture in step 2. To make this recipe vegan, use firm or extra-firm tofu instead of paneer.

Methi Roti page 110

6
Breads, Rice, and Other Grains

Naan

PREP TIME: 20 minutes, plus 1 hour to rise

COOK TIME: 15 minutes   TOTAL TIME: 1 hour 35 minutes

This is the most popular bread served in Indian restaurants. Traditionally, naan is made in a hot clay oven, called a tandoor, which provides its smoky flavor and charred texture. But a few simple techniques, such as using a pizza stone under a high broiler, give almost similar results in a home kitchen. Serve with any of the paneer curries in chapter 3 or lentil curries in chapter 5. SERVES 6

4 cups all-purpose flour

1 tablespoon instant dry yeast

2 teaspoons sugar

1 teaspoon salt

1 teaspoon onion seeds (nigella seeds)

½ cup **Yogurt** (page 168)

¾ to 1 cup lukewarm water

3 tablespoons vegetable or canola oil, or Ghee (page 167)

Melted ghee or butter, for spreading

1. In a large mixing bowl, whisk together the flour, yeast, sugar, salt, and onion seeds. Make a well in the middle of the flour and add the yogurt, ½ cup of water, and the oil. Mix until a shaggy dough forms, adding more water if necessary to incorporate all the dry ingredients. Knead the dough for 6 to 8 minutes or until a smooth, pliable dough forms. Place the dough in a lightly greased bowl, cover it, and set it aside for 1 hour.

2. Preheat the oven broiler on high with the oven rack 6 inches from the top. If using a pizza stone, place it in the oven to preheat. Lightly grease a baking sheet.

3. Divide the dough into 12 equal portions. Work with 1 portion at a time and keep the rest covered. On a lightly floured surface, roll the dough portion into a 7- to 8-inch oval naan. Brush off any excess flour. Place the naan on the prepared baking sheet. Repeat with the remaining dough portions. Place the baking sheet in the oven to broil. If using a pizza stone, then transfer the naan carefully to the preheated stone.

4. Broil for 1½ to 2 minutes, or until the tops are lightly browned. Carefully flip the naan and broil for another 1 minute. Remove the baking sheet from the oven. Brush the naan liberally with ghee and keep them warm while you cook the remaining naan. Serve warm.

Tip: To make garlic naan: Heat ¼ cup of ghee or oil in a small saucepan over medium heat. Add 4 finely minced garlic cloves and 3 tablespoons of chopped cilantro. Cook until the garlic turns golden, 2 to 3 minutes. Turn off the heat and set the pan aside. Brush the garlic ghee on the naan just before baking.

Methi Roti

PREP TIME: 15 minutes, plus 15 minutes to rest

COOK TIME: 20 minutes   TOTAL TIME: 50 minutes

Roti, or chapati, is a simple unleavened flatbread that is the most common bread made in Indian homes. Making a perfect roti comes with a little bit of practice. This methi roti is a delicious variation on regular plain roti. Adding chopped fenugreek leaves (methi) adds tons of flavor to the roti. Serve with Raita (page 169) or any pickle in chapter 7. SERVES 4

2 cups atta flour (see Glossary, page 183)

1 cup finely chopped fenugreek leaves (methi)

1 teaspoon salt

¼ teaspoon ground turmeric

½ teaspoon cayenne pepper

½ teaspoon cumin seeds

2 tablespoons vegetable or canola oil

½ to ¾ cup warm water

Melted Ghee (page 167) **or butter, for brushing**

1. In a medium bowl, combine the atta flour, fenugreek, salt, turmeric, cayenne, cumin seeds, and oil. Mix to combine. Add the oil and ½ cup of water, and mix until a fairly stiff dough forms. Knead the dough in the bowl or on a lightly floured surface until smooth. Place the dough in a lightly greased bowl, cover it, and set it aside for 15 to 20 minutes.

2. Divide the dough into 8 to 10 equal portions. Work with 1 portion at a time and keep the remaining portions covered. Lightly flour the work surface and roll the dough out into a 6- to 7-inch circle. Brush off any excess flour from the dough.

3. Heat a tawa or griddle over medium-high heat. Place the dough circle carefully on the hot pan and cook for 1 to 2 minutes per side, or until brown spots start to form on the bottom and bubbles start to appear on the surface. Remove the roti from the pan and brush it with ghee. Keep the cooked roti warm while you make the remaining roti.

Tip: To make plain roti, use atta flour, salt, oil, and water to make the dough. Then follow the recipe as written.

Missi Roti

PREP TIME: 20 minutes, plus 15 minutes to rest

COOK TIME: 20 minutes   TOTAL TIME: 55 minutes

This flavorful unleavened flatbread hails from the desert state of Rajasthan. It is made with a combination of chickpea flour and atta (Indian whole-wheat flour). Chickpea flour is naturally gluten-free, so adding whole-wheat flour makes it easier to knead into a dough. Serve missi roti with any of your favorite stir-fries or dal. SERVES 4

1 ½ cups chickpea flour (besan)

1 cup atta flour (see Glossary, page 183)

1 teaspoon salt

¾ teaspoon cayenne pepper

½ teaspoon ground cumin

¼ teaspoon ground turmeric

½ teaspoon caraway seeds (ajwain)

3 scallions, finely chopped

2 teaspoons vegetable or canola oil, plus more for brushing

¾ to 1 cup water

1. In a medium bowl, sift together the chickpea flour, atta, and salt. Add the cayenne, cumin, turmeric, caraway seeds, scallions, and oil. Mix in ¾ cup water and knead the dough until smooth. Place the dough in a lightly greased bowl, cover it, and set it aside for 15 to 20 minutes.

2. Divide the dough into 8 equal portions. Work with 1 portion at a time and keep the remaining portions covered.

3. Lightly flour the work surface and roll one dough portion into a 6- to 7-inch circle. Brush off any excess flour from the dough.

4. Heat a griddle or heavy-bottomed frying pan over medium-high heat. Place a dough circle carefully on the hot pan and cook for 2 minutes per side, or until brown spots start to form on the bottom and bubbles start to appear on the surface. Remove the roti from the pan and brush it with oil. Keep the cooked roti warm while you make the remaining roti.

Paratha

PREP TIME: 15 minutes, plus 20 minutes to rest
COOK TIME: 20 minutes **TOTAL TIME:** 55 minutes

Paratha is a flaky unleavened bread that is liberally brushed with ghee. These are slightly more time-consuming to make than Methi Roti (page 110) and hence are generally made only for special occasions. This recipe is for a basic paratha with no stuffing. The dough is layered with ghee or oil to give the flatbread a flakier texture. Serve with a paneer curry from chapter 3 or any side dish from chapter 5. **MAKES 8 PARATHAS**

2 cups atta flour (see Glossary, page 183)

½ teaspoon salt

2 tablespoons Ghee (page 167), **or vegetable or canola oil, plus more for brushing**

½ cup lukewarm water

1. In a large mixing bowl, sift the flour and salt together. Make a well in the center and add the ghee and water. Mix with a wooden spoon until the dough starts to leave the sides of the bowl, adding more water as needed. The dough should not be too dry or too sticky. Knead the dough on a lightly floured surface for 3 to 4 minutes until it is smooth and pliable. Place it in a lightly greased bowl, cover it, and set it aside to rest for 20 minutes.

2. Divide the dough into 8 equal portions. Work with 1 portion at a time and keep the remaining portions covered with a kitchen towel. On a lightly floured surface, roll out each portion into a 6-inch circle. Brush a thin layer of ghee on the dough. Fold the circle in half and brush the top with a layer of ghee. Fold it again into quarters. Now, roll out the dough into a thin triangle three times its original size. Brush off the excess flour. Keep the finished triangles covered while you work on rolling out the remaining dough.

3. Heat a griddle or heavy-bottomed frying pan over medium-high heat. Carefully place a dough triangle on the griddle and cook for 1 to 2 minutes, or until light brown spots start to form on the bottom. Turn the paratha over and cook for another minute. Make sure to not overcook the paratha; the cooking and turning process should be quick to ensure that the parathas stay soft. Keep cooked parathas covered with a kitchen towel while you cook the rest. Serve warm.

Tip: To make lachcha paratha: In step 2, after rolling the dough into a 6-inch circle, brush it with ghee, then roll it up tightly into a log. Wind the log into a coil and pinch the end underneath the coil. Roll the coil into a 6-inch circle. Continue with the recipe from step 3.

Aloo Paneer Paratha

PREP TIME: 20 minutes   COOK TIME: 30 minutes   TOTAL TIME: 50 minutes

This is a delicious variation of the popular aloo paratha. Grated paneer is added to the filling, making this bread protein-packed and a complete meal. Making stuffed paratha takes a little patience and practice, but they are well worth the effort. Serve them with Raita (page 169) or a pickle from chapter 7. **MAKES 8 PARATHAS**

2 cups atta flour (see Glossary, page 183)

1½ teaspoons salt, divided

3 tablespoons Ghee (page 167), **plus more for brushing**

½ to ⅔ cup water

2 medium potatoes, peeled and boiled

1 cup paneer, store-bought or homemade (page 170), **grated**

¾ teaspoon cayenne pepper

½ teaspoon dried mango powder (amchur)

½ teaspoon Chaat Masala (page 166)

1 teaspoon Garam Masala (page 164)

3 tablespoons finely chopped fresh cilantro

1. In a large bowl, mix together the atta flour and ½ teaspoon salt. Add the ghee and mix it into the flour for 1 to 2 minutes or until the mixture looks like coarse sand. Add ½ cup of water, mix, and knead until a smooth, pliable dough forms, adding more water as needed.

2. Cover the dough with plastic wrap and set it aside for 15 to 20 minutes.

3. In a medium bowl, mash the potatoes until smooth. Add the paneer, cayenne, remaining salt, mango powder, chaat masala, garam masala, and cilantro. Mix well and divide the mixture into 8 lemon-size portions. Shape the portions into balls. Set aside.

4. Heat a heavy-bottomed griddle or skillet over medium heat.

5. Divide the dough into 8 equal portions. Work with 1 portion of dough at a time and keep the rest covered with a kitchen towel. On a lightly floured surface, roll one dough portion out into a 4-inch circle. Place 1 ball of filling in the center of the dough circle and bring the edges of the dough over to completely cover the filling. Pinch the edges to seal. Gently roll the stuffed paratha into a 6- to 7-inch circle. Repeat with the remaining dough portions and balls of filling.

6. Place 1 paratha on the hot pan and cook for 1 to 2 minutes, or until brown spots start to form on the bottom. Turn it over and cook for a further 1 to 2 minutes. Brush the top with ghee, turn the paratha over again, and cook for another 1 minute. Brush the other side with ghee and cook until brown. Keep the cooked paratha warm and repeat with the remaining parathas.

Tips: Make sure the dough is soft and pliable. Dry dough makes preparation of parathas difficult. After stuffing the parathas, roll them out carefully without too much pressure to avoid squeezing the filling out.

Bhatura

PREP TIME: 20 minutes, plus 1 hour, 10 minutes for resting
COOK TIME: 15 minutes   TOTAL TIME: 1 hour, 45 minutes

These puffy leavened breads, served with Chana Masala (page 82), are a popular offering in Indian restaurants. Bhatura are similar to Poori (page 120) but are made with all-purpose flour and leavened with baking powder, baking soda, and yogurt. Serve them hot for the best taste. **MAKES 12 BHATURA**

1 cup Yogurt (page 168)

½ cup water, divided

2 tablespoons vegetable or canola oil, plus more for deep-frying

3 cups all-purpose flour

1 teaspoon salt

1 teaspoon baking powder

½ teaspoon baking soda

1. In a measuring cup, combine the yogurt, ¼ cup of water, and the oil. Whisk well and set aside.

2. In a large bowl, combine the flour, salt, baking powder, and baking soda. Make a well in the center and pour in the yogurt mixture. Using a wooden spoon, mix until a stiff dough forms, adding up to ¼ cup more water if needed. Using your hands, knead the dough for 4 to 5 minutes until it is smooth. Lightly grease the top of the dough. Cover the dough and set it aside for at least 1 hour, or up to 4 hours.

3. When you are ready to make the bhatura, divide the dough into 12 equal portions. Roll all 12 portions into balls and place them on a plate, cover the plate with a kitchen towel, and set the dough balls aside for 10 minutes.

4. After the resting period, roll each dough ball into a 5-inch long oval that is ¼ inch thick. Place the ovals on a baking sheet until all the dough is rolled out.

5. Fill a small wok or heavy-bottomed skillet 2 inches deep with oil and heat it over medium-high heat to 350°F. Carefully slide 1 bhatura into the hot oil, making sure to not let it fold. It will sizzle up immediately. Using the back of the slotted spoon, gently push the bhatura into the oil to let it puff up. Slowly turn it over and cook for a few more seconds to lightly brown. Use the slotted spoon to transfer the bhatura to a paper towel–lined plate. Serve right away.

Dosa

PREP TIME: 20 minutes, plus 16 to 18 hours for soaking and fermenting
COOK TIME: 15 minutes   TOTAL TIME: 16 hours, 35 minutes

Dosa is a quintessential South Indian breakfast item. It is made with rice and black lentils that are soaked and ground to a smooth batter. The batter is then left to ferment until frothy, which results in lacy and crispy dosa. The hands-on work to make dosa is quick, so don't let the long soaking and fermenting times deter you from making these wonderful breads. Leftover dosa batter will stay fresh in the refrigerator for up to a week. Serve with Sambar (page 87) and Coconut Ginger Chutney (page 136) or Peanut Chutney (page 145). **MAKES 12 DOSA**

½ cup dried, skinned whole black lentils (urad dal)

1 teaspoon fenugreek seeds (methi)

2 cups basmati or other long-grain rice

1½ to 2¼ cups of cold water, divided

1 teaspoon salt

Vegetable or canola oil, for drizzling

1. In a medium bowl, combine the lentils and fenugreek seeds with enough water to cover them by 2 to 3 inches. In a separate medium bowl, cover the rice with water to cover by 1 to 2 inches. Soak for at least 6 hours or overnight.

2. Drain the lentils and fenugreek seeds. Blend them until smooth, adding ½ cup of cold water a little at a time. Transfer the mixture to a large bowl.

3. Drain the rice and blend it until smooth, adding ½ to ¾ cup of cold water. Depending on the capacity of the blender, this might have to be done in batches. Pour the rice batter into the bowl with the lentil mixture. Using clean hands, mix the batter until well combined. The batter should be thick.

4. Cover the bowl with a lid and a kitchen towel and place it in a warm place for 10 to 12 hours. The batter should look frothy and its volume should increase. If you live in a warm area, this will happen in 8 to 10 hours, but in colder regions, this might take up to 16 hours.

5. Add ½ cup of water to the batter to get it to pouring consistency. It should resemble crêpe batter. Add the salt and mix well.

6. Heat a nonstick griddle over medium heat. Pour a ladleful of batter into the middle of the pan and use the back of the ladle to quickly spread it in a circular motion into a thin crêpe. Drizzle oil around the edges of the dosa. Cook until the bottom is crispy and browned, 1 minute. Using a thin spatula, carefully turn the dosa and cook for another 30 seconds. Remove from the griddle and serve hot. Repeat with the remaining batter.

Tip: To make restaurant-style masala dosa at home, sprinkle 1 teaspoon of Chutney Powder (page 173) on the dosa and top it with ¼ cup of Aloo Besan Subzi (page 64). Fold the dosa to cover the filling and serve it hot off the griddle.

Poori

PREP TIME: 20 minutes, plus 20 minutes to rest
COOK TIME: 15 minutes   TOTAL TIME: 55 minutes

Poori is one of the most beloved breads in India. Kids and grownups equally enjoy these puffy, melt-in-the-mouth deep-fried breads. The dough used to make poori is slightly stiff and should be prepared at least 30 minutes ahead of time. The oil should be hot so the poori puff up well. Serve with Aloo Besan Subzi (page 64) or Chana Masala (page 82). MAKES 10 POORI

2 cups atta flour (see Glossary, page 183)

½ teaspoon salt

2 tablespoons vegetable or canola oil, plus more for coating and deep-frying

½ cup water

1. In a medium bowl, sift together the flour and salt. Add the oil and rub it into the flour with your fingers. Add enough water to make a stiff but pliable dough. Knead for 3 to 4 minutes until the dough is smooth. Rub the dough with additional oil to coat and place it in a lightly greased bowl. Cover the bowl and set the dough aside to rest for at least 20 minutes.

2. Divide the dough into 10 equal portions. Roll each ball into a thin, 4-inch circle. Place the dough circles on a large plate and keep them covered with a kitchen towel.

3. Fill a small wok or heavy-bottomed skillet 2 inches deep with oil and heat it over medium-high heat to 350°F. Carefully slide 1 poori into the hot oil. It will sizzle up immediately. Using the back of a slotted spoon, gently push the poori into the oil to let it puff up. Slowly turn it over and cook for a few seconds more to lightly brown. Use the slotted spoon to transfer the poori to a paper towel-lined plate. Repeat with the remaining dough circles. Serve poori piping hot.

Basmati Rice

PREP TIME: 5 minutes, plus 30 minutes for soaking
COOK TIME: 20 minutes   TOTAL TIME: 55 minutes

This simple yet flavorful basmati rice can be served with any Indian meal and is very common in North Indian homes. Soaking basmati rice helps it keep its shape and remain as individual grains even after cooking. Serve with your favorite stir-fry or curry. SERVES 4

1 ½ **cups basmati rice**

3 cups water

1 teaspoon salt

1. Put the rice in a fine mesh sieve and rinse it 2 or 3 times, or until the water runs clear. Drain the rice and transfer it to a medium saucepan. Pour in the water and soak the rice for at least 30 minutes.

2. Stir in the salt and bring the mixture to a boil over medium-high heat. Lower the heat, cover the pan with a lid, and cook until the rice is tender, 12 to 15 minutes. Do not stir the rice while it is cooking.

3. Once all the water has evaporated, gently fluff the rice with a fork. Remove it from the heat, cover it, and set it aside for at least 5 minutes before serving.

Khichdi

PREP TIME: 10 minutes, plus 30 minutes for soaking
COOK TIME: 30 minutes   TOTAL TIME: 1 hour 10 minutes

Every region of India has its own version of this rice and lentil porridge. It is so popular that the British made their own adaptation, kedgeree, which is eaten as a breakfast dish in England. This version is made with skinned split mung beans and basmati rice. Feel free to add vegetables to make it even more wholesome. Serve with Raita (page 169) and any pickle from chapter 7. SERVES 4

½ cup dried split skinned
  mung beans (moong dal)

1 cup basmati rice

2 tablespoons Ghee
  (page 167)

½ teaspoon cumin seeds

4 whole cloves

1 (1-inch) piece
  cinnamon stick

1 medium onion,
  thinly sliced

2 teaspoons peeled grated
  fresh ginger

2 green chile peppers,
  finely chopped

½ cup green peas

1 teaspoon salt

2 tablespoons freshly
  squeezed lemon juice

2¾ cups hot water

1. Soak the lentils and rice in 2 cups of cold water for 30 minutes. Drain and set aside.

2. Heat the ghee in a heavy-bottomed saucepan over medium heat. Add the cumin seeds, cloves, and cinnamon, and cook for 30 seconds or until fragrant. Add the onion, ginger, and green chiles, and cook until the onion is lightly browned around the edges, 4 to 5 minutes.

3. Add the rice and lentils and toss to coat them evenly in the ghee. Add the peas, salt, lemon juice, and water. Bring the mixture to a boil over high heat, then lower the heat to very low, cover the pan, and cook for 15 to 20 minutes or until all the water has been absorbed and the rice is cooked. Remove the pan from the heat and allow the khichdi to rest for 5 to 10 minutes before fluffing it with a fork. Serve hot.

Pulao

PREP TIME: 5 minutes, plus 30 minutes for soaking
COOK TIME: 20 minutes   **TOTAL TIME:** 55 minutes

This simple, no-fuss pilaf is a perfect side dish for any paneer, vegetable, or lentil dish. This recipe is the basic version and it can be jazzed up in many ways. Add mixed vegetables (carrot, green beans, broccoli, peas, etc.), beans, tofu, or paneer—the options are endless. SERVES 4

1 ½ cups basmati rice

2 tablespoons Ghee
(page 167)

4 green cardamom pods

2 whole cloves

4 black peppercorns

1 teaspoon cumin seeds

1 teaspoon salt

1 tablespoon chopped mint leaves

1. Rinse the rice under cold water until the water runs clear. Transfer the rice to a bowl with 2¾ cups of water and set it aside to soak for 30 minutes.

2. Heat the ghee in a medium saucepan over medium heat. Add the cardamom, cloves, peppercorns, and cumin seeds and cook, stirring, for 1 minute or until the spices are fragrant.

3. Drain the rice, reserving the water, and add the rice to the pan. Stir-fry for 2 to 3 minutes.

4. Add the reserved water and salt and bring to a boil over high heat. Reduce the heat to low, cover the pan, and cook until all the water has been absorbed and the rice is tender, 12 to 15 minutes. Remove the pan from the heat and set it aside, covered, for 5 minutes. Gently fluff the rice with a fork, sprinkle it with the mint, and serve.

Vegetable Biryani

PREP TIME: 20 minutes, plus 30 minutes for soaking

COOK TIME: 45 minutes   **TOTAL TIME:** 1 hour 35 minutes

Biryani is a special Sunday dish in most Indian households. The flavorful casserole with layers of rice and spicy mixed vegetables is cooked in a heavy pan with a tight lid to seal in all the delicious flavors. This hearty dish is generally served with Raita (page 169) and Kachumber (Cucumber Salad, page 140). SERVES 6

2 cups basmati rice

3 tablespoons vegetable or canola oil, divided

1 bay leaf

4 whole cloves

3 cardamom pods

1 (1-inch) piece cinnamon stick

2½ teaspoons salt, divided

1 teaspoon cumin seeds

1 large onion, thinly sliced

2 green chile peppers, chopped

2 teaspoons Ginger-Garlic Paste (page 172)

3 cups chopped mixed vegetables (carrot, peppers, green beans, corn, etc.)

1 cup tomato puree

¼ teaspoon ground turmeric

1 teaspoon cayenne pepper

1 teaspoon ground cumin

1. Wash the rice in a strainer under cold running water until the water runs clear. Transfer the rice to a medium bowl, cover it with water, and soak for at least 30 minutes. Drain and set aside.

2. Fill a large saucepan with water and add 1 tablespoon of oil and the bay leaf, cloves, cardamom, cinnamon, and 1 teaspoon of salt. Bring the water to a rolling boil on high heat. Lower the heat to medium-high and add the drained rice. Cook for 7 to 8 minutes or until the rice is cooked but still has a bite. Drain the rice in a large colander and set it aside to cool.

3. Heat the remaining 2 tablespoons of oil in a large heavy-bottomed skillet over medium heat. Add the cumin seeds and, once they start to change color, add the onion, green chiles, and ginger-garlic paste, and cook until the onion is lightly browned around the edges, 5 to 6 minutes. Add the mixed vegetables and cook, covered, until they are tender, 10 to 12 minutes.

1 teaspoon ground
coriander

1 teaspoon Garam Masala
(page 164)

½ cup **Yogurt** (page 168)

¼ **cup finely chopped mint
leaves, divided**

¼ **cup finely chopped
cilantro leaves and
tender stems, divided**

1 **cup store-bought fried
onions, divided** (optional)

4. Stir in the tomato puree, turmeric, cayenne, cumin, coriander, garam masala, and the remaining 1½ teaspoons of salt. Cover and cook for 4 to 5 minutes. Add the yogurt and mix well to combine. Cook for 2 minutes. Add 1 tablespoon each of mint and cilantro. Mix well and turn off the heat. Taste and adjust the seasoning.

5. Transfer half of the vegetable mixture to a small bowl.

6. On the remaining vegetable mixture in the skillet, evenly spread half the rice. Sprinkle the rice layer evenly with 1 tablespoon each of mint and cilantro and ½ cup of fried onions (if using). Spread the reserved vegetable mixture in an even layer on top, followed by the remaining rice. Sprinkle with the remaining mint, cilantro, and fried onions. Cover the skillet with a tight-fitting lid and cook on very low heat for 12 to 15 minutes, or until the rice is completely cooked through and the flavors have mingled. Serve hot.

Tip: To make great-tasting biryani, make sure that all the layers are well seasoned. Taste as you go and adjust the seasonings before layering the dish.

Spicy Seviyan (Indian-Style Vermicelli)

PREP TIME: 10 minutes   **COOK TIME:** 20 minutes   **TOTAL TIME:** 30 minutes

Seviyan, or thin vermicelli, is made from wheat flour and is available in Indian groceries. It can be used to make both savory and sweet dishes. This spicy seviyan can be served for breakfast or for lunch. My mom used to make this for us as an after-school snack. Feel free to use whatever vegetables you have on hand or skip them altogether for a super quick and easy version. **SERVES 4**

2 tablespoons Ghee
(page 167), **or vegetable or canola oil, divided**

1 cup vermicelli/seviyan

½ teaspoon mustard seeds

½ teaspoon cumin seeds

2 green chile peppers, sliced

2 teaspoons peeled grated fresh ginger

1 medium onion, sliced

1 small green bell pepper, finely chopped

½ cup green peas

½ cup corn kernels

1 tomato, finely chopped

¼ teaspoon cayenne pepper

¼ teaspoon Garam Masala
(page 164)

1 teaspoon salt

2 cups hot water

1 tablespoon freshly squeezed lemon juice

1. Heat 1 tablespoon of ghee in a large nonstick skillet over medium heat. Add the vermicelli and cook, stirring, until it turns a shade darker, 3 to 4 minutes. Transfer the vermicelli to a bowl and set it aside.

2. In the same skillet, heat the remaining 1 tablespoon of ghee. Add the mustard and cumin seeds and cook until the seeds start to splutter, about 30 seconds. Add the green chiles and ginger and cook for another 30 seconds. Stir in the onion and bell pepper and cook until the veggies are tender, 4 to 5 minutes.

3. Add the peas, corn, tomato, cayenne, garam masala, and salt. Cook until the tomato is tender, 3 minutes. Add the hot water and bring the mixture to a boil over high heat. Stir in the vermicelli, lower the heat, cover the skillet, and cook until all the water has been absorbed, 6 to 8 minutes. Mix in the lemon juice and serve hot.

Tip: If seviyan is unavailable, use thin spaghetti or capellini noodles that are broken into 2- to 3-inch pieces.

Vegetable Fried Rice

PREP TIME: 15 minutes   **COOK TIME:** 10 minutes   **TOTAL TIME:** 25 minutes

Vegetable fried rice is a popular street food in India because it is inexpensive and fast to make. It is also a colorful and flavorful dish that is perfect for using up any leftover rice. You can use freshly made rice, but make sure to cool it to room temperature before using it in this recipe. Serve this dish with Chile Paneer (page 42) or Gobi Manchurian (page 19) for a delicious home-made Indo-Chinese meal. **SERVES 6**

3 tablespoons vegetable or canola oil

1 tablespoon peeled grated fresh ginger

3 garlic cloves, minced

1 small onion, chopped

2 green chile peppers, sliced

1 small carrot, diced

10 to 12 green beans, trimmed and finely chopped

½ cup green peas

1 cup thinly sliced cabbage

6 scallions, chopped

1 tablespoon soy sauce

1 teaspoon salt

¼ teaspoon freshly ground black pepper

2 teaspoons vinegar

4 cups cooked basmati rice, at room temperature

1 tablespoon freshly squeezed lemon juice

2 tablespoons finely chopped fresh cilantro

1. Heat the oil in a large wok or skillet over medium-high heat. Add the ginger and garlic and cook for 30 to 45 seconds or until they smell fragrant. Add the onion, green chiles, carrot, green beans, peas, and cabbage, and cook until the veggies are crisp-tender, 4 to 5 minutes. Add the scallions, soy sauce, salt, pepper, and vinegar, and mix well. Cook for 1 minute.

2. Add the rice and stir-fry for 1 minute. Stir in the lemon juice and cilantro. Taste and adjust the seasoning. Serve hot.

Tip: To make this a wholesome one-pot meal, add paneer or tofu with the vegetables, or scramble 3 or 4 eggs and add them at the very end.

Yogurt Rice

PREP TIME: 10 minutes, plus 30 minutes for soaking
COOK TIME: 30 minutes   TOTAL TIME: 1 hour 10 minutes

Many South Indian people think that a meal is incomplete if yogurt is not served at the end, so this yogurt rice gets featured quite often in Indian homes. Like Vegetable Fried Rice (page 127), this recipe is also a great way to use up leftover rice. Add grated carrot, cucumber, or pomegranate arils for color and an extra layer of flavor. Serve with the Nimboo Achaar (Lemon Pickle) from page 138. SERVES 6

1 cup basmati rice

1 tablespoon vegetable or
   canola oil

½ teaspoon mustard seeds

1 teaspoon split skinned
   black lentils (urad dal)

1 teaspoon yellow split
   peas (chana dal)

1 dried red chile
   pepper, broken

⅛ teaspoon
   asafetida (hing)

6 to 8 fresh curry leaves

2 green chile
   peppers, sliced

⅛ teaspoon ground
   turmeric

¾ teaspoon salt

1½ cups Yogurt
   (page 168), whisked

1. Wash the rice in a strainer under cold running water until the water runs clear. Transfer the rice to a medium bowl, cover it with water, and soak it for at least 30 minutes. Drain.

2. Combine the rice with 2 cups of water in a medium saucepan and bring it to a boil over high heat. Lower the heat, cover the pan, and cook until all the water has been absorbed and the rice is cooked through, 18 to 20 minutes. Turn off the heat and keep the pan covered for 10 to 15 minutes before fluffing the rice with a fork.

3. Heat the oil in a small skillet over medium heat. Add the mustard seeds, lentils, split peas, and red chile, and cook until the mustard seeds start to splutter, 30 to 45 seconds. Add the asafetida, curry leaves, and green chiles, and cook for 1 minute. Add the turmeric and salt, and turn off the heat.

4. Pour the yogurt into a large bowl and stir in the lentil mixture. Next, add the cooked rice and mix well. Serve at room temperature or chilled.

Upma (Spicy Semolina Porridge)

PREP TIME: 10 minutes   **COOK TIME:** 15 minutes   **TOTAL TIME:** 25 minutes

Upma is a quick and easy breakfast, lunch, or snack. My version is packed with vegetables, but feel free to add your favorite veggies or skip them altogether for a classic plain upma. For a touch of indulgence, add a generous dollop of Ghee (page 167) on top before serving. Serve with Coconut Ginger Chutney (page 136). SERVES 4

1 tablespoon vegetable or canola oil

1 teaspoon mustard seeds

2 teaspoons yellow split peas (chana dal)

2 teaspoons split skinned black lentils (urad dal)

3 tablespoons cashews, broken

1 dried red chile pepper, broken

6 fresh curry leaves

1 medium onion, finely chopped

2 teaspoons peeled grated fresh ginger

2 green chile peppers, halved lengthwise

1 small potato, peeled and finely diced

1 small carrot, peeled and finely diced

½ cup frozen peas (no need to thaw)

3 cups water

1 teaspoon salt

1 cup Cream of Wheat cereal (sooji/semolina)

1. Heat the oil in a medium saucepan over medium heat. Add the mustard seeds and, once they start to splutter, add the split peas, lentils, cashews, dried red chile, and curry leaves. Cook for 1 minute or until the lentils and cashews are golden.

2. Add the onion, ginger, and green chiles, and cook for 3 to 4 minutes or until the onion turns translucent. Add the potato, carrot, and green peas, and cook for 5 minutes or until the veggies are almost tender.

3. Add the water and salt and bring the mixture to a boil. Lower the heat and stir in the cereal. Cover and cook for 3 to 4 minutes or until all the water has been absorbed. Serve warm.

Mango Chutney page 133

7

Chutneys, Pickles, and Salads

Tomato Chutney

PREP TIME: 15 minutes   COOK TIME: 25 minutes   TOTAL TIME: 40 minutes

This is the most common chutney made in India. Fresh tomatoes are cooked until mushy and then spiced with cayenne pepper, ground fenugreek seeds, and garlic. This is a great recipe to use when tomatoes are ripe and fresh. The chutney can be made ahead of time and stored in the refrigerator for up to 2 weeks. MAKES 2 CUPS

2 teaspoons fenugreek seeds

¼ cup vegetable or canola oil, divided

3 medium tomatoes, chopped

1 tablespoon tamarind concentrate

2 teaspoons cayenne pepper

2 teaspoons salt

2 teaspoons mustard seeds

4 garlic cloves, thinly sliced

1. In a small saucepan over medium heat, dry roast the fenugreek seeds until toasted and fragrant, 2 to 3 minutes. Remove from the heat and let cool. Grind to a fine powder in a spice grinder and set aside.

2. Heat 2 tablespoons of oil in a heavy-bottomed saucepan over medium heat. Add the tomatoes and cook, stirring occasionally, until they are soft, 6 to 8 minutes.

3. Add the tamarind, cayenne, and salt, and cook until the mixture thickens, 10 to 12 minutes. Remove the pan from the heat and stir in the fenugreek powder. Mix well.

4. Heat the remaining 2 tablespoons of oil in a small saucepan over medium heat. Add the mustard seeds and garlic, and cook until the seeds start to splutter and the garlic turns golden, 2 to 3 minutes. Pour the hot oil into the tomato mixture. Mix well and let cool completely. Store in a clean, airtight glass container.

Tip: Use either vine-ripe or Roma tomatoes in this recipe because they are juicy and have an intense flavor.

Mango Chutney

PREP TIME: 10 minutes   COOK TIME: 40 minutes   TOTAL TIME: 50 minutes

This sweet, spicy, and tart chutney can be served with everything. It is very easy to make and provides a beautiful contrast to savory dishes. It also goes well with Papad (page 21), Paratha (page 112), or Methi Roti (page 110). Look for firm but ripe mangoes to make this chutney. MAKES 1 CUP

2 medium firm, ripe mangoes

1 tablespoon vegetable or canola oil

2 teaspoons peeled grated fresh ginger

2 garlic cloves, crushed

1 (1-inch) piece cinnamon stick

3 whole cloves

¾ teaspoon cayenne pepper

¼ cup raisins

¼ cup sugar

¼ cup vinegar

2 teaspoons salt

1. Wash and thoroughly dry the mangoes. Peel, halve, and seed them. Cut the flesh into cubes and keep them at the ready.

2. Heat the oil in a heavy-bottomed saucepan over medium heat. Add the ginger and garlic and cook for 1 minute or until fragrant. Add the cinnamon stick, cloves, cayenne, raisins, sugar, vinegar, and chopped mango. Bring to a boil.

3. Lower the heat and simmer for 25 to 30 minutes or until the mango is thick and pulpy, like jam. Add the salt and mix well. Taste and add more cayenne, if needed. Remove the whole spices.

4. Store the chutney in clean, dry jars with tight-fitting lids in a cool place or in the refrigerator.

Cilantro Mint Chutney

PREP TIME: 10 minutes

This is an Indian version of pesto. It is spicy, herby, and refreshing. This chutney is usually served with Samosas (page 12), Tikki Chaat (page 15), or Vada Pav (page 24), but it is also delicious with Methi Roti (page 110) or Naan (page 108). MAKES 2 CUPS

2 cups cilantro leaves and tender stems

1 cup mint leaves

1 teaspoon peeled grated fresh ginger

1 garlic clove (optional)

2 green chile peppers

2 tablespoons freshly squeezed lemon juice

½ teaspoon sugar

½ teaspoon salt

2 tablespoons water

1. Combine the cilantro, mint, ginger, garlic (if using), green chiles, lemon juice, sugar, salt, and water in a blender and blend into a smooth paste, adding more water if the chutney looks too thick.

2. Store in an airtight container in the refrigerator for up to 1 week.

Tip: Cilantro mint chutney can be stored in the freezer for up to 2 months. Fill an ice cube tray with the chutney and freeze until set. Transfer the cubes to a resealable plastic bag and store in the freezer. Thaw and use as needed.

Tamarind Chutney

PREP TIME: 10 minutes   COOK TIME: 25 minutes   TOTAL TIME: 35 minutes

This sweet and sour chutney is a quintessential accompaniment to appetizers and street food. Sour tamarind is combined with sweet dates and jaggery (or brown sugar) to make this chutney. Cayenne pepper adds a nice balance with its spiciness. Serve with Samosas (page 12) and Tikki Chaat (page 15) to add lip-smacking flavor. MAKES 2 CUPS

2 cups dates, seeded and chopped

¼ cup tamarind concentrate

½ cup jaggery (or brown sugar)

1 teaspoon cayenne pepper

⅛ teaspoon asafetida (hing)

½ teaspoon salt

3 cups water

1. In a medium saucepan over medium-high heat, combine the dates, tamarind, jaggery, cayenne, asafetida, salt, and water. Bring the mixture to a boil. Lower the heat and simmer for 20 to 25 minutes or until the dates are soft and turning mushy.

2. Let the mixture cool completely. Transfer the mixture to a blender and blend it into a smooth paste. Strain through a sieve to remove any strings or seeds. Store in an airtight container in the refrigerator for up to 3 weeks.

Coconut Ginger Chutney

PREP TIME: 10 minutes   **COOK TIME:** 5 minutes   **TOTAL TIME:** 15 minutes

Coconut chutney is a quintessential South Indian accompaniment to Dosa (page 118) or Upma (page 129). But this chutney also goes really well with Methi Roti (page 110) and even Khichdi (page 122). It is best eaten the day it is made, although leftovers can be stored for 1 day. **MAKES 2 CUPS**

2 cups grated fresh or frozen coconut

2 teaspoons peeled grated fresh ginger

1 green chile pepper

1 teaspoon tamarind concentrate

½ cup cilantro leaves and tender stems

1 tablespoon unsalted, roasted peanuts

1 teaspoon salt

¼ cup water

2 teaspoons vegetable or canola oil

1 teaspoon split black lentils (urad dal)

½ teaspoon mustard seeds

1 dried red chile pepper, broken

6 curry leaves

1. Combine the coconut, ginger, green chile, tamarind, cilantro, peanuts, and salt in a blender. Blend into a smooth paste with the water. Transfer the mixture to a serving bowl.

2. Heat the oil in a small saucepan over medium heat. Add the lentils, mustard seeds, and dried chile, and cook until the mustard seeds start to splutter and the lentils have turned golden, 1 minute. Add the curry leaves and remove the saucepan from the heat. Add this hot oil to the coconut chutney and mix well. Serve right away.

Tip: If you cannot find fresh coconut, shredded dried unsweetened coconut can be used. Soak it in warm water for 15 to 20 minutes to reconstitute and then use it in the recipe.

Aam ka Achaar (Mango Pickle)

PREP TIME: 15 minutes **COOK TIME:** 5 minutes **TOTAL TIME:** 20 minutes

Mango is considered the king of fruits in India. Raw mango is used widely to make pickles, summer drinks such as Aam Panna (page 150), and more. This quick and easy mango pickle is spicy and finger-licking good. Make sure to use clean, dry spoons for serving to maintain its freshness. Mango pickle can be served with just about any recipe in chapter 6. **MAKES 3 CUPS**

2 large green unripe mangoes, peeled, pitted, and cut into ½-inch cubes

2 tablespoons cayenne pepper

1½ tablespoons salt

¼ cup vegetable or canola oil

2 teaspoons mustard seeds

½ teaspoon fenugreek seeds

½ teaspoon asafetida (hing)

1. In a medium bowl, combine the mangoes, cayenne, and salt.

2. Heat the oil in a small saucepan over medium heat. Add the mustard seeds and fenugreek seeds and, once the seeds start to splutter, add the asafetida and mix well. Stir the hot oil into the mango mixture and mix well. Cool the pickle completely before transferring to a clean jar. Store in a cool place or the refrigerator for up to 2 weeks.

Nimboo Achaar (Lemon Pickle)

PREP TIME: 5 minutes   COOK TIME: 15 minutes   TOTAL TIME: 20 minutes

This spicy, lemony pickle is quick and easy to make, and enhances the taste of plain or stuffed Parathas (page 112 and 114), Khichdi (page 122), or Yogurt Rice (page 128). Choose thin-skinned lemons, organic if you can. Floral Meyer lemons will work beautifully in this recipe. Lemon achaar tastes better the next day after the lemons and spices have had a chance to mellow each other out. SERVES 6

2 medium lemons, washed and each cut into 16 wedges

¾ cup water

¼ ground turmeric

1 tablespoon salt

1½ tablespoons cayenne pepper

½ teaspoon ground roasted fenugreek seeds

3 tablespoons vegetable or canola oil

1 teaspoon mustard seeds

½ teaspoon asafetida (hing)

1. Combine the lemon wedges, water, turmeric, and salt in a medium saucepan. Bring to a boil over medium-high heat. Lower the heat and simmer for 8 to 10 minutes or until the lemons are tender. Remove the pan from the heat. Add the cayenne and fenugreek and mix well.

2. Heat the oil in a small saucepan over medium heat. Add the mustard seeds and asafetida and, once the seeds start to splutter, add the hot oil mixture to the lemons. Mix well.

3. Let the pickle cool completely before storing it in a clean glass container in the refrigerator for up to 2 weeks.

Tip: Thin-skinned lemons absorb the flavors easily and are less bitter.

Green Chile Pickle

PREP TIME: 15 minutes

This is an Indian version of pickled jalapenos, although this version is more spicy than tangy. It is widely made in North India and served with Methi Roti (page 110) and Khichdi (page 122). Remove the seeds from some of the peppers to tone down the spiciness, or substitute less-spicy jalapeños for the serrano peppers. **MAKES 2 CUPS**

2 teaspoons
mustard seeds

8 to 10 medium green
serrano peppers

¼ cup freshly squeezed
lemon juice

2 teaspoons salt

2 tablespoons vegetable or
canola oil

¼ teaspoon ground
turmeric

⅛ teaspoon
asafetida (hing)

1. Grind the mustard seeds into a powder in a spice grinder or with a mortar and pestle.

2. Wash and thoroughly dry the chile peppers. Leave them on a kitchen towel to make sure they are completely dry. Cut the peppers into ¼-inch-thick, round slices.

3. Put the sliced chiles in a medium mason jar along with the mustard powder, lemon juice, and salt.

4. Heat the oil in a small saucepan over medium heat. Add the turmeric and asafetida. Turn off the heat and add the hot oil to the chiles. It is best to let the flavors mingle for at least 1 day before serving. Store it in the refrigerator for up to 1 month.

Kachumber (Cucumber Salad)

PREP TIME: 10 minutes, plus 30 minutes to chill   TOTAL TIME: 40 minutes

This is arguably the most popular salad throughout India. It is refreshing, easy to make, and goes really well with any meal. If using regular cucumbers, peel them before chopping. Julienned beets can be added to the salad to add color and crunch. The salad can be made ahead of time and refrigerated until ready to serve. SERVES 4

2 medium English cucumbers, finely chopped

2 medium tomatoes, chopped

4 scallions, chopped

1 green chile pepper, finely chopped

1 tablespoon finely chopped fresh cilantro

1 tablespoon finely chopped fresh mint

2 tablespoons freshly squeezed lemon juice

½ teaspoon salt

In a medium bowl, combine the cucumbers, tomatoes, scallions, green chile, cilantro, mint, lemon juice, and salt. Toss well and refrigerate for at least 30 minutes. Serve chilled.

Chana Chaat (Chickpea Salad)

PREP TIME: 15 minutes

I love salads that are hearty and filling, and this chickpea salad fits the bill perfectly. It is protein-packed from the beans and chock full of flavor and colorful vegetables. Add some toasted Naan (page 108) to make the salad more substantial, or use it as a filling in a sandwich or wrap. **SERVES 6**

2 cups cooked chickpeas

1 small cucumber, peeled and diced

1 medium tomato, seeded and diced

1 teaspoon salt

1 green chile pepper, finely chopped (optional)

2 tablespoons freshly squeezed lemon juice

1 tablespoon finely chopped fresh cilantro

1 teaspoon Chaat Masala (page 166)

¼ cup pomegranate arils

1. In a medium bowl, combine the chickpeas, cucumber, and tomato, and toss well.

2. Add the salt, green chile (if using), lemon juice, cilantro, chaat masala, and pomegranate arils, and mix well. Refrigerate for at least 1 hour before serving.

Raw Mango Salad

PREP TIME: 10 minutes   **COOK TIME:** 5 minutes   **TOTAL TIME:** 15 minutes

Raw mango salad is a popular street food in India during summer. It is crunchy, crispy, and very refreshing. I have added toasted peanuts and cashews for even more crunch. Raisins add a nice, sweet bite. This salad is best when eaten right away. **SERVES 4**

3 tablespoons peanuts

2 tablespoons cashews

1 raw green unripe mango, peeled, seeded, and diced

1 small red onion, finely chopped

3 tablespoons raisins

1 tablespoon Cilantro Mint Chutney (page 134)

2 tablespoons lime juice

½ teaspoon salt

2 tablespoons finely chopped fresh cilantro

1. In a small skillet over medium heat, roast the peanuts and cashews until they are lightly browned. Remove the nuts from the pan and let them cool slightly. Coarsely chop the nuts and set them aside.

2. In a medium bowl, combine the mango, onion, raisins, and roasted nuts, and toss well. Add the chutney, lime juice, salt, and cilantro. Mix well. Taste and adjust the seasonings. Serve immediately.

Laccha (Onion-Tomato Salad)

This salad is served in most Indian restaurants. The layers of thinly sliced onion, tomatoes, and cucumber make it a very colorful and inviting dish. Marinating the onion in salt makes it less spicy and more crispy. Serve this salad right after making it. SERVES 6

1 medium red onion, cut into thin rings

½ teaspoon salt, plus more for sprinkling

½ teaspoon ground cumin

¼ teaspoon cayenne pepper

2 medium tomatoes, thinly sliced

2 medium cucumbers, peeled and thinly sliced

2 tablespoons freshly squeezed lemon juice

½ teaspoon Chaat Masala (page 166)

¼ teaspoon ground pepper

1. Combine the onion and salt in a colander or sieve and allow to sit for 15 minutes. Rinse under cold water, then drain thoroughly and transfer to a medium bowl.

2. Add the cumin and cayenne to the onions and toss well.

3. On a serving platter, arrange the tomato slices in a layer and top with the cucumber slices, then the onions. Drizzle with the lemon juice and sprinkle with the chaat masala, salt, and pepper. Serve immediately.

Radish Salad

PREP TIME: 10 minutes   COOK TIME: 5 minutes   TOTAL TIME: 15 minutes

This is a beautifully fresh and colorful salad that is very quick and easy to make. The tempering adds a lot of flavor. Coarsely chopped peanuts give a crunchy texture and balance the hot flavor of the radishes. Choose the smallest, freshest looking radishes to make this salad and serve it with any Indian meal. SERVES 4

2 cups small red radishes, trimmed and cut into quarters

1 tablespoon vegetable or canola oil

¼ teaspoon cumin seeds

¼ teaspoon mustard seeds

⅛ teaspoon asafetida (hing)

¼ teaspoon ground turmeric

¼ teaspoon salt

2 teaspoons freshly squeezed lemon juice

½ cup unsalted, roasted peanuts, coarsely chopped

1. Put the radishes in a small bowl.

2. Heat the oil in a small saucepan over medium heat. Add the cumin seeds and mustard seeds and, once the seeds start to splutter, add the asafetida, turmeric, and salt, and turn off the heat. Let the oil mixture cool slightly, then stir in the lemon juice.

3. Add the oil to the radishes along with the peanuts. Toss well to thoroughly mix all the ingredients. Serve immediately.

Peanut Chutney

PREP TIME: 10 minutes   **COOK TIME:** 5 minutes   **TOTAL TIME:** 15 minutes

This is one of my absolute favorite chutneys. Roasted peanuts are ground with garlic, chile, tamarind, and cilantro. The tamarind adds a nice tangy flavor. Serve this creamy chutney with Dosa (page 118), Methi Roti (page 110), or Khichdi (page 122). MAKES 1 CUP

¾ cup roasted, unsalted peanuts

2 garlic cloves, minced

1 green chile pepper, chopped

¼ cup chopped fresh cilantro leaves

2 teaspoons tamarind concentrate

½ teaspoon salt

⅓ cup water

2 teaspoons vegetable or canola oil

½ teaspoon mustard seeds

1 dried red chile pepper, broken

6 curry leaves

1. Combine the peanuts, garlic, green chile, cilantro, tamarind, salt, and water in a blender. Blend into a smooth puree, adding more water if the mixture looks too thick. Taste and adjust the seasonings. Transfer the peanut mixture to a small bowl.

2. Heat the oil in a small saucepan over medium heat. Add the mustard seeds and, once they start to splutter, add the dried chile and curry leaves. Cook for 30 seconds, then add the hot oil to the peanut mixture. Mix well and serve immediately.

Tip: You can roast peanuts at home in a dry skillet over medium heat until they are evenly browned on all sides. Stir frequently to avoid burning them. If all you have on hand are roasted, salted peanuts, then use them and omit adding the salt in this recipe.

Falooda page 159

8
Drinks and Sweets

Masala Chai

PREP TIME: 5 minutes   **COOK TIME:** 10 minutes   **TOTAL TIME:** 15 minutes

Most Indians start their day with a hot cup of milky chai, the Indian version of tea. In this version, whole spices and black tea leaves or black tea bags are simmered in a milk-water mixture until aromatic. Whole milk gives the best texture to the chai, but nonfat or low-fat milk would work well, too. Add sugar in the amount you like just before serving, and serve the chai piping hot. SERVES 4

2 cups water

3 tablespoons loose black tea or 3 black tea bags

2 whole cloves

2 cardamom pods, crushed

3 black peppercorns

2 cups whole milk

1 to 2 tablespoons sugar

1. In a medium saucepan over medium-high heat, combine the water, tea, cloves, cardamom, and peppercorns, and bring to a boil.

2. Add the milk and bring the mixture to a boil again. Make sure that the milk does not boil over. Reduce the heat to medium-low and simmer for 2 to 3 minutes, stirring occasionally.

3. Strain the tea through a very fine sieve into 4 serving cups. Discard the spices and tea in the sieve.

4. Stir in the sugar and serve hot.

Tip: To add an extra spicy kick to chai, add 2 teaspoons coarsely crushed ginger to the water along with the spices, and simmer. Then follow the recipe as written.

Sweet and Savory Lassi

PREP TIME: 10 minutes

This yogurt-based drink can be made either sweet or savory. Both versions are cooling, refreshing, and perfect with a spicy Indian meal. These basic recipes can be jazzed up in many ways. Add fresh fruit such as strawberries, bananas, or peaches to the sweet version, or spices and herbs to the savory version. Always serve lassi chilled. **SERVES 4**

For sweet lassi

3 cups Yogurt (page 168)

1 cup milk

1½ tablespoons sugar

¼ teaspoon ground cardamom

1 cup crushed ice

For savory lassi (masala lassi)

3 cups yogurt

1 cup water

1 teaspoon salt

1 teaspoon ground cumin

¼ cup finely chopped fresh cilantro

2 tablespoons chopped fresh mint leaves

1 cup crushed ice

To make sweet or savory lassi

Combine all the ingredients in a blender and blend until the mixture is smooth and frothy. Pour into 4 serving glasses and enjoy.

Tip: To make the popular mango lassi, use the flesh of 2 medium fresh ripe mangos or 2 cups canned mango puree. Blend the mango with 1½ cups yogurt, ½ cup milk, 1 cup crushed ice, and ½ teaspoon ground cardamom into a smooth mixture. Serve immediately.

Aam Panna (Green Mango Drink)

PREP TIME: 10 minutes   COOK TIME: 30 minutes   TOTAL TIME: 40 minutes

As much as Indians love to eat fresh ripe mangos, they also love sour, unripe green mangoes. They are used in various recipes such as the spicy Aam ka Achaar (page 137) or this drink. Aam panna is a sweet and sour drink that is so refreshing on a hot summer day. Double or triple the recipe to make extra concentrate, store it in the refrigerator for up to 1 month, and have it on hand to enjoy anytime. SERVES 6

- **2 medium raw unripe green mangoes, peeled, seeded, and chopped**
- **½ cup brown sugar**
- **1 teaspoon ground cumin**
- **¼ teaspoon salt**
- **½ teaspoon ground cardamom**
- **4 cups water, divided**
- **¼ cup mint leaves, for garnish** (optional)

1. In a medium saucepan over medium-high heat, combine the mango, sugar, cumin, salt, cardamom, and 1 cup of water. Bring the mixture to a boil. Lower the heat and simmer until the sugar has dissolved and the mango is very tender, 15 to 20 minutes. Cool the mixture.

2. Transfer the mango mixture to a blender and add the remaining 3 cups of water. Blend to a smooth consistency. If the pulp looks too stringy, strain the mixture through a fine sieve. Transfer the aam panna concentrate to a clean jar or bottle and refrigerate it until ready to serve.

3. To serve, fill a glass three-quarters full with aam panna and the rest with cold water. Mix well and serve cold, garnished with mint leaves (if using).

Besan Ladoo

PREP TIME: 10 minutes, plus 20 minutes to cool

COOK TIME: 25 minutes   TOTAL TIME: 55 minutes

Ladoo is a quintessential celebratory Indian dessert and is made for every special occasion, from weddings to housewarmings. There are many variations, but this recipe is made with chickpea flour (besan), hence the name besan ladoo. Roasting the chickpea flour with ghee on low heat makes it very aromatic and flavorful. Care must be taken while roasting the flour to avoid burning it; slow and steady roasting will make for the best-tasting ladoo. SERVES 10

¼ **cup Ghee** (page 167)

1 **cup chickpea flour (besan), sifted**

2 **tablespoons chopped pistachios or almonds**

½ **cup confectioners' sugar**

¼ **teaspoon ground cardamom**

1. In a heavy-bottomed pan on low heat, melt the ghee. Add the chickpea flour and stir it into the melted ghee. Initially, it will have the consistency of coarse sand.

2. Cook the mixture, stirring constantly. After 20 to 25 minutes of constant stirring, ghee will start to ooze out of the flour. The mixture will thin at this point and the flour will be golden brown and aromatic. It should be smooth and not clumpy. Remove the mixture from the heat and transfer it to a bowl. Set it aside to cool for 15 to 20 minutes.

3. In the meantime, dry roast the nuts in a small skillet over medium-low heat until they are golden brown, about 5 minutes. Let the nuts cool slightly and add them to the chickpea flour mixture.

4. After the roasted chickpea flour has cooled for 20 minutes, add the sugar and cardamom to the bowl. Mix well. The mixture should be smooth and dough-like. Divide the mixture into 10 to 12 equal pieces and roll each piece into a ball. Place the balls on a plate to cool completely. Serve at room temperature.

Mango Kulfi

PREP TIME: 5 minutes, plus 4 hours to chill
COOK TIME: 20 minutes   TOTAL TIME: 4 hours, 25 minutes

Kulfi is Indian ice cream. It is said that this frozen treat was brought to India by Mughals hundreds of years ago. Kulfi comes in a wide variety of flavors. This recipe is flavored with mango puree and is one of my family's favorites. It is easy to make and does not need churning. The only special equipment needed is an ice pop mold. Cornstarch prevents the formation of icicles and makes the frozen kulfi creamy and decadent. SERVES 6

1 (12-ounce) can
  evaporated milk
  (1 ½ cups)

½ cup heavy cream

¼ cup milk

1 teaspoon cornstarch

3 tablespoons sugar

½ cup mango puree,
  homemade or
  store-bought

½ teaspoon ground
  cardamom

1. In a medium heavy-bottomed saucepan over medium heat, combine the evaporated milk and cream. Bring the mixture to a boil, stirring frequently to avoid scorching the bottom. Simmer for 2 minutes.

2. In a small bowl, combine the milk and cornstarch into a thick slurry. Add the cornstarch mixture to the saucepan and cook, stirring constantly, for 2 minutes.

3. Whisk in the sugar and mango puree and cook for 3 to 4 minutes, or until the mixture has slightly thickened. Stir in the cardamom, mix well, turn off the heat, and let the mixture cool completely. Pour it into kulfi or ice pop molds and freeze for at least 4 hours. When ready to serve the kulfi, remove the molds from the freezer and briefly run them under hot water to unmold. Serve immediately.

Tip: If you have good-quality sweet mangoes, then definitely use them, but I find store-bought canned mango puree to be more reliable in this recipe. Kesar or Alphonso canned mango puree are my go-to options.

Gulab Jamun

PREP TIME: 10 minutes   COOK TIME: 15 minutes, plus 1 hour to soak
TOTAL TIME: 1 hour, 25 minutes

Gulab jamun, which is probably the most beloved Indian dessert, was brought to India by the Mughals. The name literally means "rose-flavored plum." This juicy, fried dough dessert is made with dry milk powder and fried until golden brown before being soaked in a rosewater-flavored sugar syrup. So good! Serve warm or chilled. SERVES 6

1 cup sugar

1 cup water

½ teaspoon rose water

½ cup dry milk powder, preferably full-fat

3 tablespoons all-purpose flour

2 teaspoons semolina flour

½ teaspoon baking soda

1 tablespoon Ghee (page 167)

2 to 3 tablespoons milk

Vegetable oil, canola oil, or ghee, for deep-frying

1. In a medium saucepan over medium-high heat, combine the sugar and water. Bring to a boil. Lower the heat and simmer for 2–3 minutes. Stir in the rose water and turn off the heat. Keep the sugar syrup warm while you make the jamun.

2. In a small mixing bowl, combine the milk powder, all-purpose flour, semolina flour, and baking soda. Mix well. Add the ghee and milk, 1 tablespoon at a time, and mix with your fingers or a spoon into a soft dough. Knead the dough gently until it is smooth. Divide the dough into 12 equal portions and roll each portion into a smooth ball. Set the balls aside.

3. Fill a medium wok or Dutch oven 2 inches deep with oil and heat it over medium-high heat to 350°F. Gently slide the balls into the hot oil and cook, stirring occasionally, until they are evenly golden brown all over. Use a slotted spoon to transfer the balls to the warm sugar syrup. Set aside for at least 1 hour to let the jamun soak up the syrup. Serve warm or chilled.

Tip: If rose water is not available, use ¼ teaspoon ground cardamom.

Gajar Halwa (Carrot Halwa)

PREP TIME: 15 minutes   **COOK TIME:** 45 minutes   **TOTAL TIME:** 1 hour

This is one of the simplest Indian desserts to make, yet it is creamy, rich, and decadent. Traditionally, this is made with red carrots called gajar, *which are available during winter and are much sweeter than regular orange carrots. However, halwa is delicious no matter which carrot you use. Grating the carrots is the only somewhat labor-intensive part of this recipe, and I usually employ an enthusiastic family member to help. If that is not an option, use a food processor to grind the carrots into a coarse paste. Serve the halwa warm with a dollop of vanilla ice cream. It can also be served chilled.* SERVES 6

¼ cup **Ghee** (page 167) **or unsalted butter**

6 medium carrots, peeled and grated (4 cups)

2 cups full-fat milk

½ **teaspoon ground cardamom**

¾ **cup sugar**

2 tablespoons chopped cashews

2 tablespoons chopped pistachios

2 tablespoons golden raisins

1. In a large skillet over medium heat, melt the ghee. Add the carrots. Mix well to coat the carrots with ghee and cook, stirring occasionally, until the carrots do not smell raw anymore, 8 to 10 minutes.

2. Stir in the milk and cardamom and simmer until the carrots are cooked through, stirring occasionally, 15 to 20 minutes. Most of the milk should have been absorbed by this point.

3. Add the sugar, cashews, pistachios, and raisins, and cook for another 8 to 10 minutes or until the sugar has melted. Cook, stirring occasionally, until the halwa thickens, about 5 minutes.

Tips: Leftovers can be refrigerated in an airtight container for up to 1 week and can be frozen for up to 1 month.

Kheer

PREP TIME: 5 minutes, plus 30 minutes to soak
COOK TIME: 45 minutes   **TOTAL TIME:** 1 hour 20 minutes

Kheer is a classic example of the extremely popular milk-based desserts in India. It is a simple Indian version of rice pudding made with just a handful of ingredients. Care must be taken while cooking the rice to ensure that the bottom does not scald. Serve this creamy dessert warm or chilled. SERVES 4

¼ **cup long-grain rice**

4 **cups whole milk**

¼ **cup sugar**

¼ **teaspoon ground cardamom**

2 **tablespoons chopped cashews**

2 **tablespoons raisins**

1. Wash the rice under running water, then soak it in a bowl of water for at least 30 minutes.

2. In a medium heavy-bottomed saucepan over medium-high heat, bring the milk to a boil, stirring frequently to avoid scorching the bottom. Drain the rice and add it to the milk. Lower the heat to medium-low and simmer for 30 to 35 minutes until the rice is tender and the milk is creamy and thickened. Stir the mixture occasionally, scraping the bottom and mixing the cream forming on the top into the milk.

3. Stir in the sugar, cardamom, cashews, and raisins. Mix well and cook for another 8 to 10 minutes. Serve warm or chilled.

Badam Burfi (Almond Fudge)

PREP TIME: 5 minutes   **COOK TIME:** 15 minutes   **TOTAL TIME:** 20 minutes

Burfi, an Indian version of fudge, has many variations depending on the region and ingredients. This recipe is made with almonds and is one of the simplest burfi recipes. This is one of the few Indian desserts that is not milk-based and can easily be made vegan. For a delicious variation, cashews or a combination of nuts can be used in this recipe. **SERVES 10**

½ cup sugar

¼ cup water

1 cup almond flour

1 teaspoon Ghee (page 167) or vegetable oil

¼ teaspoon ground cardamom

1. Lightly grease a plate and cut a 12-inch long piece of parchment paper.

2. In a medium skillet over medium-high heat, combine the sugar and water and bring the mixture to a boil. Once the mixture boils, lower the heat to medium-low and stir in the almond flour. Using a wooden spoon, stir the mixture continuously to make sure that there are no lumps. Cook, still stirring continuously, until the mixture starts to come away from the sides of the pan, about 5 minutes.

3. Stir in the ghee and cardamom and cook for 3 to 4 minutes, stirring continuously. When the mixture starts to look a little dry, around the 8-minute mark, carefully take a tiny piece of the mixture and roll it. If it rolls into a non-sticky ball, it is ready. If not, cook for another 2 minutes and test again.

4. Transfer the cooked almond mixture to the greased plate and let it cool for 4 to 5 minutes. While it is still warm, knead the mixture into a smooth dough. Place the dough on one half of the parchment paper and fold the other half over it. Using a rolling pin, roll the dough into a ⅛-inch-thick rectangle. Score the rolled dough into equal squares or diamonds. Let the burfi cool completely before storing it in an airtight container for up to 1 week.

Tip: To make almond flour at home, blend 1¼ cups blanched almonds into a coarse powder. Sift it through a fine-mesh sieve to remove any bigger pieces and measure 1 cup to use in the recipe.

Shrikhand

PREP TIME: 5 minutes, plus 1 hour to chill   TOTAL TIME: 1 hour, 5 minutes

This is a yogurt-based dessert from Gujarat, a northwestern state in India. Traditionally, shrikhand is made by straining yogurt to make it thick and creamy, but I find that full-fat Greek yogurt, which is naturally thick, is an excellent time-saving substitute. This recipe is a basic one, flavored with saffron and cardamom. Serve this with chopped seasonal fruit for a simple dessert, or jazz it up by adding pureed fruit such as mango or strawberry. Always serve shrikhand chilled. SERVES 4

2 tablespoons warm milk

½ teaspoon saffron strands, crushed

2 cups plain full-fat Greek yogurt

½ cup confectioners' sugar

½ teaspoon ground cardamom

¼ cup roasted unsalted almonds, coarsely chopped

¼ cup roasted unsalted pistachios, coarsely chopped

1. In a small bowl, combine the milk with the saffron. Mix well and set aside.

2. In a medium bowl, whisk the yogurt and sugar together until the mixture is well-combined and airy. Add the cardamom and cooled saffron milk and mix until incorporated. Add almost all the roasted almonds and pistachios, reserving some for garnish. Refrigerate the yogurt for at least 1 hour. Sprinkle the chilled yogurt with the reserved nuts and serve. Leftovers can be refrigerated for up to 4 days.

Tip: If you plan to use homemade plain Yogurt (page 168), place it in a cheesecloth- or muslin-lined colander and allow it to drain for at least 6 to 8 hours in the refrigerator. Make sure to place the colander in a large bowl to avoid a mess..

Falooda

PREP TIME: 20 minutes   COOK TIME: 20 minutes   TOTAL TIME: 20 minutes

Falooda is a work of art due to its beautiful layers of colors and textures. It is a treat to look at and an even bigger treat to enjoy all the different flavors. Basil seeds add a nice texture and mellow flavor to this drink. They are readily available in Indian groceries, but if you cannot find them, use chia seeds instead. SERVES 4

2 teaspoons basil or chia seeds

¼ cup water

½ cup falooda noodles, or yellow cellophane or glass noodles, cut into 2-inch pieces

¼ cup rose syrup, plus 4 tablespoons

1½ cups chilled whole milk

4 scoops vanilla ice cream, for topping (optional)

Roasted unsalted almonds or pistachios, coarsely chopped (optional)

1. In a small bowl, soak the basil seeds in the water and set them aside for 20 to 30 minutes or until they are swollen.

2. While the seeds are soaking, prepare the noodles according to the package instructions. Drain and rinse them with cold water to stop their cooking. Set the noodles aside.

3. In a small bowl, mix the rose syrup with the milk.

4. To serve, pour 1 tablespoon of rose syrup into the bottom of each of 4 serving glasses. Divide the noodles evenly between the glasses. Top the noodles with a tablespoon of soaked basil seeds. Divide the rose milk between the glasses. Top each with a scoop of vanilla ice cream and sprinkle with chopped nuts, if using. Serve immediately.

Tip: Rose syrup is a rose-flavored pink syrup that is available in Indian and Middle Eastern grocery stores.

Fruit Custard

PREP TIME: 5 minutes, plus 3 hours to chill   COOK TIME: 10 minutes

Seasonal fruit served with creamy custard is the most popular way to serve fruit in India. Eggs are rarely used in Indian desserts, due to the lacto-vegetarian diet followed by many Indians. So, custard that traditionally uses eggs is made with cornstarch here instead. You can use commercially available custard powder with added flavors to make this dessert, but cornstarch works just as well. Use any of your favorite seasonal fruits. Serve chilled. SERVES 6

2½ tablespoons cornstarch

3 cups whole milk, divided

¼ cup sugar

½ teaspoon vanilla extract

1 medium banana, chopped

1 cup red or green grapes, halved

¼ cup chopped strawberries

¼ cup pomegranate arils

1. In a small bowl, whisk the cornstarch into ¼ cup of milk, making sure that there are no lumps. Set the mixture aside.

2. In a medium heavy-bottomed saucepan over medium heat, combine the remaining milk and sugar and bring the mixture to a boil, stirring frequently. Once the milk comes to a rolling boil, lower the heat. Add the cornstarch mixture in a steady stream while whisking continuously. Cook for 1 to 2 minutes, stirring and scraping the bottom to avoid scorching, until the mixture is thick and creamy. Turn off the heat, stir in the vanilla, and mix well.

3. Transfer the custard to a bowl and place a piece of plastic wrap right on top of the custard to prevent a skin forming on top. Chill the mixture for at least 3 hours. The custard will thicken as it cools.

4. To serve, divide the custard evenly among 6 serving bowls, top each with banana, grapes, strawberries, and pomegranate, and serve right away.

Vermicelli Payasam

PREP TIME: 5 minutes   **COOK TIME:** 15 minutes   **TOTAL TIME:** 20 minutes

This is a quicker but equally delicious alternative to Kheer (page 155). This dessert is made for all special occasions in our household. Vermicelli are long, thin pasta made with wheat flour and are widely available in Indian and Asian grocery stores. If vermicelli are unavailable, thin spaghetti or angel hair pasta can be used instead. Break the pasta into 1- to 2-inch pieces before cooking. Serve this dessert warm or chilled.   **SERVES 4**

4 cups whole or 2 percent milk

2 tablespoons Ghee (page 167), **divided**

2 tablespoons chopped raw cashews

2 tablespoons chopped pistachios

2 tablespoons raisins

½ cup vermicelli or seviyan

½ cup sugar

⅛ teaspoon ground cardamom

1. In a heavy-bottomed saucepan over medium heat, heat the milk, stirring it occasionally to prevent scorching. Bring the milk to a slow boil.

2. In the meantime, heat 1 tablespoon of ghee in a small skillet and add the cashews, pistachios, and raisins. Cook, stirring continuously, until the nuts turn golden and the raisins are plump. Transfer the mixture to a small bowl and set aside.

3. In the same skillet over medium-low heat, combine the remaining 1 tablespoon of ghee and the vermicelli. Cook, stirring frequently, until the vermicelli is golden brown and smells fragrant. Remove the skillet from the heat.

4. Once the milk comes to a boil, add the roasted vermicelli to it and cook until the vermicelli is tender, 4 to 5 minutes. Stir in the sugar and cardamom and cook for another 3 to 4 minutes, until the sugar has melted and the mixture starts to thicken a little. Add the nut-and-raisin mixture and stir to combine. Serve warm or chilled.

Cucumber Mint Raita page 169

9

Spice Blends and Other Staples

Garam Masala

PREP TIME: 5 minutes   COOK TIME: 5 minutes   TOTAL TIME: 10 minutes

Garam masala *literally means "warming spice mix" and is probably the most widely used spice blend in Indian cooking. It is a mixture of whole or ground spices, and each region has its own blend. It is best to make your own masala because store-bought versions do not have as much flavor as freshly made ones.* MAKES ¼ CUP

Seeds from
  8 cardamom pods

1 tablespoon cumin seeds

2 teaspoons
  coriander seeds

2 dried bay leaves

½ teaspoon whole cloves

1 (1-inch) piece
  cinnamon stick

½ teaspoon black
  peppercorns

In a small skillet over medium-low heat, dry roast all the spices, stirring frequently, until they are aromatic, 1 to 2 minutes. Transfer the spices to a bowl and allow them to cool completely. Grind the spices in a spice grinder to a fine powder. Store garam masala in an airtight jar for up to 1 month.

Tandoori Masala

PREP TIME: 5 minutes

A tandoor is an Indian-style clay oven that is typically used to cook Naan (page 108). This tandoori masala is a spice blend used to marinate meat or vegetables that are to be cooked in the tandoor. It has a spicy, smoky taste that accentuates the flavors imparted by the oven. Try the Paneer Tikka recipe (page 35), where the marinated paneer is grilled to achieve the same smoky flavor as cooking in a tandoor. MAKES 1 CUP

¼ **cup cayenne pepper**

¼ **cup garlic powder**

2 **tablespoons freshly ground black pepper**

1 **tablespoon Chaat Masala** (page 166)

3 **tablespoons Garam Masala** (page 164)

3 **tablespoons dried fenugreek leaves (kasoori methi)**

1 **tablespoon salt**

In a blender, combine the cayenne, garlic powder, pepper, chaat masala, garam masala, fenugreek, and salt, and blend the mixture to a fine powder. Store Tandoori Masala in an airtight container for up to 1 month.

Chaat Masala

PREP TIME: 5 minutes   **COOK TIME:** 5 minutes   **TOTAL TIME:** 10 minutes

Chaat masala is a unique spice blend with salty, tangy, and spicy flavors. It is generally used in snacks such as Bhel Puri (page 26) and Vegetable Pakora (page 14), but it can also be used in salad dressings, fruit juices, or even sprinkled on fruit and vegetables as a seasoning. **MAKES ½ CUP**

3 tablespoons
    coriander seeds

2 tablespoons cumin seeds

2 teaspoons salt,
    preferably black salt

1 tablespoon dried mango
    powder (amchur)

1 teaspoon
    cayenne pepper

1 teaspoon freshly ground
    black pepper

1. In a small skillet over medium-low heat, dry roast the coriander seeds until they are aromatic. Transfer the roasted seeds to a bowl.

2. In the same skillet, roast the cumin seeds until they are aromatic. Remove the skillet from the heat.

3. In a spice grinder, grind the coriander and cumin seeds to a fine powder. Add the salt, mango powder, cayenne, and black pepper, and blend until the mixture is well combined. Store Chaat Masala in an airtight jar for up to 1 month.

Ghee

PREP TIME: 5 minutes   COOK TIME: 20 minutes   TOTAL TIME: 25 minutes

Dairy products have a special place in Indian cuisine and are part of the daily diet. Ghee is basically clarified butter. It has a nutty flavor that adds a unique taste to many curries and desserts. MAKES 1½ CUPS

1 pound unsalted butter

1. In a heavy-bottomed saucepan over medium-low heat, melt the butter. Bring the butter to a simmer, stirring occasionally. The butter will foam initially, but the foam will subside as the butter simmers.

2. The milk solids will start to settle to the bottom of the pan and will slowly turn a rich golden-brown color. This will take 15 to 20 minutes.

3. Once the ghee turns clear with a golden hue, turn off the heat.

4. Carefully pour the ghee through a fine mesh strainer lined with cheesecloth into a clean, dry, 2-cup mason jar. Discard the milk solids and set the ghee aside to cool completely before covering the jar with a lid.

Tip: Ghee can be stored at room temperature for up to 2 months. It will last longer when stored in the refrigerator.

Yogurt

PREP TIME: 5 minutes   **COOK TIME:** 5 minutes, plus 8 to 10 hours to set
TOTAL TIME: 8 hours 10 minutes

Yogurt is very easy to make at home; most Indians set their own almost every day because yogurt is a part of everyday meals in many regions. All you need to make homemade yogurt is milk and an active yogurt culture. When making yogurt for the first time, buy store-bought yogurt that contains live cultures. I use whole milk because I feel that the resulting yogurt has the best flavor and texture. Lower-fat (2 percent and 1 percent) milk can also be used, but the texture and mouthfeel will be slightly different. **MAKES 2½ CUPS**

2½ cups milk
2 tablespoons plain yogurt

1. In a heavy-bottomed saucepan over medium heat, bring the milk to a boil. Remove the pan from the heat and allow the milk to cool to lukewarm.

2. Whisk the yogurt until it is smooth, then stir it into the warm milk until they are well combined.

3. Cover the pan and place it in a warm, draft-free area.

4. The yogurt should be thick and set in 8 to 10 hours.

Tip: A turned-off oven or the microwave work very well for making yogurt in areas with cold weather. Leave the oven light on in winter to create a warm environment.

Cucumber Mint Raita

PREP TIME: 10 minutes

Raita is a yogurt-based accompaniment served with almost every Indian meal. It acts as a contrast to hot and spicy dishes and soothes the digestive tract. Raitas are very versatile. Any vegetable, fruit, legume, or herb can be added to yogurt to make a raita. This cucumber raita is a commonly made recipe. It is great to serve with Vegetable Biryani (page 124) or Aloo Paneer Paratha (page 114). **SERVES 4**

1 cup Yogurt
(page 168), **whisked**

¾ teaspoon salt

1 medium English cucumber, seeded and grated

¼ cup finely chopped fresh mint

½ teaspoon cumin seeds, toasted and ground

1 green chile pepper, finely chopped

In a medium bowl, combine the yogurt, salt, cucumber, mint, cumin, and green chile, and mix well. Taste and adjust the seasonings. Chill the raita until serving time. Raita will keep well in the refrigerator for up to 3 days.

Paneer

PREP TIME: 5 minutes, plus 3 hours to firm up

COOK TIME: 20 minutes   TOTAL TIME: 3 hours, 25 minutes

Paneer is an Indian type of cheese that is quite easy to make at home by coagulating milk with vinegar. The curdled milk is drained to let the curds and whey separate, and then the cheese is pressed into blocks. Homemade paneer is creamy and mellow tasting, and is a common ingredient in many North Indian dishes such as Palak Paneer (page 40) or Paneer Makhani (page 39). MAKES 1 POUND

12 cups whole milk

3 tablespoons distilled vinegar

1. In a large saucepan over medium-high heat, bring the milk to a boil. Stir occasionally to avoid the milk sticking to the bottom of the pan.

2. Once the milk comes to a rolling boil, lower the heat and stir in the vinegar. Remove the pan from the heat and set it aside until large bits of curd start to form. Shake the pan slowly to allow the curds to form and release the whey. If the curds are slow to form, put the saucepan over low heat again for a few seconds.

3. Line a colander with cheesecloth, making sure to have an overhang on the sides. Pour the cheese and whey into the colander. Let it drain.

4. Once the cheese is cool enough to touch, gather the edges of the cheesecloth and fold them over to cover it.

5. Place a large, heavy can of tomatoes or beans on the cheesecloth-covered cheese and set it aside for 2 to 3 hours to firm up.

6. Remove the weight and unwrap the firm cheese. Use it right away or wrap it in plastic and store in the refrigerator for up to 4 days, or in the freezer for up to 2 months.

Panch Phoron

PREP TIME: 5 minutes

Panch phoron *literally means "five-spice blend." It is a very common ingredient in East Indian cooking, especially in Bengali dishes such as Bengali Masoor Dal (page 93). Unlike other masalas, this is a whole spice mix instead of a ground spice mix.* MAKES ¼ CUP

1 teaspoon cumin seeds

1 teaspoon onion seeds (nigella seeds)

1 teaspoon mustard seeds

1 teaspoon fennel seeds

1 teaspoon fenugreek seeds

Combine the cumin, nigella, mustard, fennel, and fenugreek seeds in a small bowl. Store Panch Phoron in an airtight jar for up to 4 months.

Ginger-Garlic Paste

PREP TIME: 5 minutes

Many Indian dishes call for this flavorful paste, which is very simple to make and stores well in the refrigerator. MAKES ¼ CUP

2 large knobs ginger
(8 ounces)

6 to 8 heads garlic

1. Peel and coarsely chop the ginger and garlic.

2. Combine the chopped ginger and garlic in a food processor or blender and blend until smooth. Add 2 to 3 tablespoons of water to help in grinding the mixture to a fine paste.

3. Store the ginger-garlic paste in a clean airtight jar in the refrigerator for up to 4 weeks.

Chutney Powder

PREP TIME: 5 minutes   **COOK TIME:** 15 minutes   **TOTAL TIME:** 20 minutes

Chutney powder is nearly always found on a South Indian breakfast platter. It is a nutty, spicy powder that is great with Dosa (page 118) or Upma (page 129). I sometimes use this powder as curry powder in vegetable dishes as well. MAKES 2 CUPS

½ cup dried yellow split peas (chana dal)

¼ cup split skinned black lentils (urad dal)

¼ cup raw peanuts

½ cup coriander seeds

6 dried red chile peppers

3 tablespoons dry grated unsweetened coconut

1 tablespoon tamarind concentrate

¼ teaspoon asafetida (hing)

1½ teaspoons salt

1. In a small skillet over medium-low heat, dry roast the split peas, lentils and peanuts separately until they change color slightly and start to smell fragrant. Transfer the roasted lentils and nuts to a medium bowl.

2. In the same pan, dry roast the coriander seeds and dried red chiles until they are aromatic and the chiles turn a shade darker. Add the coriander and chiles to the bowl.

3. Finally, dry roast the coconut until it is golden, 2 to 3 minutes. Add the toasted coconut to the bowl and let it cool completely.

4. Add the tamarind, asafetida, and salt to the mixture and stir to combine. Using a spice grinder, grind the mixture to a fine powder. Store chutney powder in an airtight container for up to 1 month.

Pav Bhaji Masala

PREP TIME: 5 minutes   **COOK TIME:** 15 minutes   **TOTAL TIME:** 20 minutes

Pav bhaji masala is a fragrant spice mix used in making Pav Bhaji (page 17). It gives the dish a spicy flavor and unique aroma. This masala is also a handy substitute for garam masala in vegetable or rice dishes. MAKES ¾ CUP

6 dried red chile
  peppers, broken

3 tablespoons
  coriander seeds

2 tablespoons cumin seeds

1 (2-inch) piece
  cinnamon stick

4 whole cloves

2 cardamom pods

2 teaspoons fennel seeds

1 teaspoon ground
  turmeric

1½ tablespoons dried
  mango powder (amchur)

1 teaspoon black salt

2 teaspoons freshly
  ground black pepper

1. In a small skillet over medium heat, dry roast the dried red chiles, coriander, cumin, cinnamon, cloves, cardamom, and fennel seeds until fragrant, 3 to 4 minutes.

2. Remove the spices from the pan and allow them to cool completely.

3. Combine the roasted spices with the turmeric, mango powder, black salt, and pepper. In a spice grinder, grind the mixture into a fine powder. Store this spice blend in an airtight container for up to 2 months.

Chole Masala

PREP TIME: 5 minutes   **COOK TIME:** 5 minutes   **TOTAL TIME:** 10 minutes

This spice powder gives the ever-popular Chana Masala (page 82) its characteristic flavor and aroma. This is a hot, spicy, tangy, and very flavorful spice blend. It is also used to make Tikki Chaat (page 15). **MAKES ¾ CUP**

6 dried red chile peppers

1 (2-inch) piece cinnamon stick, broken

2 cardamom pods

6 whole cloves

1 teaspoon black peppercorns

3 tablespoons coriander seeds

1½ tablespoons cumin seeds

½ teaspoon ground nutmeg

½ teaspoon dried ginger powder

2 tablespoons dried mango powder (amchur)

½ teaspoon asafetida (hing)

1 teaspoon black salt

1. In a small skillet over medium heat, dry roast the chiles, cinnamon, cardamom, cloves, peppercorns, coriander, and cumin until fragrant, 3 to 4 minutes.

2. Let the spices cool completely.

3. Combine the roasted spices with the nutmeg, ginger, mango powder, asafetida, and salt. In a spice grinder, grind the mixture to a fine powder. Store it in an airtight container for up to 4 months.

Sambar Masala

PREP TIME: 5 minutes   COOK TIME: 15 minutes   TOTAL TIME: 20 minutes

Each household in South India probably has its own sambar masala recipe. This version is mine. Sambar masala is used to make a South Indian stew called Sambar (page 87). Adding split peas to the spice powder not only adds flavor but also makes the sambar thicker. This is one of the spice blends that I always have in my pantry. MAKES 1 CUP

8 dried red chile peppers

¼ cup coriander seeds

1 tablespoon black peppercorns

2 tablespoons cumin seeds

1 teaspoon fenugreek seeds

1 teaspoon mustard seeds

¼ cup dried yellow split peas (chana dal)

1 tablespoon white poppy seeds

2 tablespoons dry grated coconut

1 (1-inch) piece cinnamon stick

10 to 12 fresh curry leaves

1 teaspoon ground turmeric

1. In a small skillet over medium heat, dry roast each ingredient separately until it is aromatic. Transfer each as it is roasted to the same medium bowl and allow all the spices to cool completely.

2. In a spice grinder, grind the mixture into a fine powder. Store the masala in an airtight container for up to 2 months.

Chana Saag page 86

Menu Ideas

Everyday Lunch

- Palak Dal, page 90
- Masala Cabbage, page 67
- Basmati Rice (page 121) or Plain Roti (see Tip, Methi Roti recipe, page 110)
- Aam ka Achaar (Mango Pickle), page 137
- Raita, such as Cucumber Mint Raita (page 169)

Everyday Dinner

- Bengali Masoor Dal (page 93)
- Zucchini Dry Curry (page 76)
- Plain Paratha (page 112)
- Kachumber (Cucumber Salad), page 140
- Yogurt Rice (page 128)

Diwali/Holiday Dinner Party

- Mango Lassi (see Tip, Sweet and Savory Lassi recipe, page 149)
- Laccha (Onion-Tomato Salad), page 143
- Garlic Naan (see Tip, Naan recipe, page 108)
- Vegetable Biryani (page 124)
- Gobi Aloo (page 56)
- Paneer Makhani (page 39)
- Raita, such as Cucumber Mint Raita (page 169)
- Gulab Jamun (page 153)

North Indian Dinner Party

- Tikki Chaat (page 15)
- Gajar Methi Subzi (Carrot and Fenugreek Sauté), page 66
- Dal Makhani (page 80)
- Pulao (page 123)
- Plain Paratha (page 112)
- Aam ka Achaar (Mango Pickle), page 137
- Raita, such as Cucumber Mint Raita (page 169)
- Kulfi, such as Mango Kulfi (page 152)

South Indian Dinner Party

- Okra Fries (page 23)
- Vegetable Korma (page 99)
- Green Bean Sauté (page 70)
- Sambar (page 87)
- Basmati Rice (page 121)
- Plain Roti (see Tip, Methi Roti recipe, page 110)
- Yogurt Rice (page 128)
- Fruit Custard (page 160)

Hearty Brunch

- Paneer Bhurji, page 52, or Anda Bhurji, page 38
- Dosa, page 118
- Aloo Besan Subzi (Potato Curry with Chickpea Flour), page 64
- Peanut Chutney (page 145)
- Masala Chai (page 148)

Indian Vegan

- Masala Papad (page 21)
- Chana Chaat (Chickpea Salad), page 141
- Panchmel Dal (Five-Lentil Stew), page 91
- Spicy Corn Stir-Fry (page 71)
- Badam Burfi (Almond Fudge), page 156

Indian Picnic

- Raw Mango Salad (page 142)
- Rajma Masala (page 83)
- Methi Roti (page 110)
- Yogurt Rice (page 128)
- Gulab Jamun (page 153)

Kid-Friendly

- Vegetable Pakora (page 14)
- Poori (Puffy Fried Breads), page 120
- Chana Masala (page 82)
- Vegetable Fried Rice (page 127)
- Mango Kulfi (page 152)

Measurement Conversions

Volume Equivalents (Liquid)

US STANDARD	US STANDARD (OUNCES)	METRIC (APPROXIMATE)
2 tablespoons	1 fl. oz.	30 mL
¼ cup	2 fl. oz.	60 mL
½ cup	4 fl. oz.	120 mL
1 cup	8 fl. oz.	240 mL
1½ cups	12 fl. oz.	355 mL
2 cups or 1 pint	16 fl. oz.	475 mL
4 cups or 1 quart	32 fl. oz.	1 L
1 gallon	128 fl. oz.	4 L

Oven Temperatures

FAHRENHEIT (F)	CELSIUS (C) (APPROXIMATE)
250°F	120°C
300°F	150°C
325°F	165°C
350°F	180°C
375°F	190°C
400°F	200°C
425°F	220°C
450°F	230°C

Volume Equivalents (Dry)

US STANDARD	METRIC (APPROXIMATE)
⅛ teaspoon	0.5 mL
¼ teaspoon	1 mL
½ teaspoon	2 mL
¾ teaspoon	4 mL
1 teaspoon	5 mL
1 tablespoon	15 mL
¼ cup	59 mL
⅓ cup	79 mL
½ cup	118 mL
⅔ cup	156 mL
¾ cup	177 mL
1 cup	235 mL
2 cups or 1 pint	475 mL
3 cups	700 mL
4 cups or 1 quart	1 L

Weight Equivalents

US STANDARD	METRIC (APPROXIMATE)
½ ounce	15 g
1 ounce	30 g
2 ounces	60 g
4 ounces	115 g
8 ounces	225 g
12 ounces	340 g
16 ounces or 1 pound	455 g

Resources

Spices and Ingredients

Kalustyan's

123 Lexington Avenue
New York, NY 10016
FoodsOfNations.com

Penzeys Spices

Multiple locations nationwide
Penzeys.com

Online Shopping

Amazon.com
IShopIndian.com
IndianFoodsCo.com
MySpiceSage.com

Cookbooks

660 Curries by Raghavan Iyer
Anjum's New Indian by Anjum Anand
Entice with Spice: Easy Indian Recipes for Busy People
by Shubhra Ramineni
Indian-ish: Recipes and Antics from a Modern American Family
by Priya Krishna
Made in India: Recipes from an Indian Family Kitchen by Meera Sodha
A Taste of India by Madhur Jaffrey

Glossary

Ajwain (caraway seeds): This spice resembles cumin seeds, but it is much smaller and much stronger in flavor, and needs to be used sparingly.

Asafetida (hing): This is a dried resin from a fennel-like plant and has a strong, pungent flavor. A little goes a long way. Buy the ground version instead of the block because it is easier to use and has a mellower taste.

Atta/chapati flour: This whole-wheat flour is used to make Indian flatbreads and is sold in Indian, Pakistani, and other Asian stores. Indian wheat is lower in protein than US wheat and is ideal for making fluffy, thin roti. If you do not have access to atta, then use half US whole-wheat flour and half all-purpose flour in recipes calling for atta.

Basil seeds (sabja): These tiny black seeds from a wild Indian basil plant are usually soaked in water until they swell. They are flavorless and are used mostly for their texture in drinks, such as Falooda (page 159).

Bay leaf (tej patta): These are the dried leaves of the cassia tree. They are mostly used whole to flavor curries and rice dishes but are also dry roasted and ground into spice blends.

Bitter melon (karela): True to its name, this pale, cucumber-like gourd with warty skin is bitter in taste. It is used to make stir-fries and curries.

Black-eyed peas (lobhia): These have a buttery, creamy taste and are easy to cook from their dry state. But canned and frozen black-eyed peas are also widely available in grocery stores and are very convenient.

Black lentils (urad dal): Black lentils come in four forms: whole, whole skinned, split, and split skinned. The whole lentils have a black skin and need to be soaked or precooked before use. The split skinned variety is cream in color and becomes glutinous and creamy when cooked.

Black salt (kala namak): Black salt has a strong sulfuric odor but a pleasant smoky taste. It is available as black or brown lumps, or ground to pinkish-gray powder, in Indian grocery stores.

Cardamom (elaichi): There are two types of cardamom used in Indian cooking: small green pods and large black pods. The green pods are very aromatic and are commonly used in many Indian dishes, especially desserts. Black pods are slightly bitter and are used mostly in North Indian dishes.

Cayenne pepper: A hot red chile powder made from sun-dried red chile peppers.

Chaat masala: This spice blend is used as seasoning for snacks known as *chaat* (which literally means "to lick" in Hindi). The spice blend is flavorful and adds a punch to dishes.

Chickpea flour (besan): Made from dried chickpeas, this pale-yellow flour is high in dietary fiber and protein. It is used to make crispy fried pakoras and to make soft missi roti.

Chickpeas (kabuli chana): These are one of the most popular and versatile legumes. They have a nutty texture and can easily absorb spices and flavors.

Chile peppers: Fresh chile peppers are an important ingredient in Indian cooking for adding heat and pungency. Generally, smaller chiles are hotter than larger ones. Dried red chiles such as cayenne or chile de arbol are also widely used in Indian cooking.

Cilantro (coriander leaves): These are used both as a garnish and as an ingredient. They stay fresh for four to five days.

Cloves (laung): Cloves have a distinctive, strong, pungent flavor. Usually used whole to flavor a dish, they are not meant to be eaten whole and can be removed before serving.

Coconut (nariyal): Coconut is widely used in Indian cooking, especially in the coastal regions. Either fresh or dried unsweetened coconut can be used in the recipes. Coconut milk is also a popular ingredient.

Coriander seeds (dhaniya): These are the round, brown seeds of the coriander plant. They are aromatic and widely used in Indian cooking. To make ground coriander, coriander seeds are dry roasted and ground to a smooth powder.

Cumin seeds (jeera): Cumin is one of the most widely used spices in Indian cooking. It is either used whole or in powder form (roasted and ground). Cumin has a warm and nutty flavor that enhances any dish.

Curry leaves (kari patta): These aromatic leaves add a distinctive flavor to many Indian dishes, especially South Indian dishes. They are available fresh all year round in Indian grocery stores.

Dal: Dal is a generic word used to describe legumes or legume-based dishes. Dal could be any type of beans, lentils, or even split peas.

Dry mango powder (amchur powder): Tart green mango slices are sun-dried and ground to a powder to make this spice. This adds a tart, sour flavor to North Indian dishes.

Fennel seeds (saunf): These oval, ridged, greenish-yellow seeds are sweetly aromatic and are available whole or ground.

Fenugreek (methi leaves): Fresh methi is sold in bunches in most Indian and Asian grocery stores along with cilantro and mint. The leaves have a slightly bitter flavor that goes well in curries. The dried version is called kasoori methi and is used in curry sauces to add a unique flavor and aroma.

Garam masala: This is the most popular Indian spice blend; it adds flavor to any dish. It is available in most grocery stores or you can make it at home (see the recipe on page 164).

Garlic (lasoon): Garlic is used extensively in Indian cooking to add assertive flavor to dishes. It is also widely used in combination with ginger in many curries and rice dishes.

Ghee: This clarified butter is very flavorful and aromatic. Ghee is one of the primary cooking fats in India. It is easy to make at home with unsalted butter or can be store-bought.

Ginger (adrak): Fresh ginger is used throughout India and is a very common ingredient. It is often ground into a paste or finely grated to be used in recipes. Look for a fresh, heavy root that snaps easily. Store in the refrigerator for up to 3 weeks or in the freezer for extended storage.

Jaggery (gur): Jaggery is raw sugar made from sugar cane (and sometimes date or palm sap); it tastes like brown sugar. It is sold as lumps and comes in various colors depending on the juice from which it is made.

Kadai: This is a deep, wok-shaped cooking pan. Cast-iron kadai are generally used for deep-frying. A nonstick or carbon steel wok is a good substitute.

Mint leaves: Fresh mint is used in marinades, chutneys, rice dishes, and curries. Spearmint is more common in Indian cooking. When buying mint, make sure that the leaves are fresh and green with no brown or black spots. I store mint like cilantro, in the refrigerator.

Mung beans (moong dal): The most common forms of mung beans are whole and split skinned. Mung beans cook fast in either form.

Mustard seeds: These tiny round seeds have a hot, pungent flavor. Mustard seeds are available in yellow, brown, or black colors and in whole or powdered form. Indian cooking uses the black type of mustard seed, also called "rai."

Onion seeds (nigella/kalonji): These black, teardrop-shaped seeds have a subtle onion flavor. They are one of the spices used in panch phoron.

Pigeon peas (toor dal): These are available in both whole and split skinned versions. All the recipes in the book use the split skinned version because they are widely available and easy to cook.

Red kidney beans: These kidney-shaped beans are very popular in North India, especially in Punjab. They have a meaty texture and aroma that work well in Rajma Masala (page 83) and Dal Makhani (page 80).

Red lentils (masoor dal): These lentils are very popular all over the world and mostly used in their split skinned form. They cook very easily and have a very smooth texture, making them perfect for soups and dals.

Rice flour: This finely ground rice is used to add crispiness to snacks. White and brown rice flours are available in well-stocked groceries and Indian stores.

Rose water (gulab jal): Made from rose essence and water, this aromatic liquid is usually added in order to perfume desserts and drinks. Use sparingly.

Saffron (kesar): Saffron is the most expensive spice in the world and is the dried stigma of a crocus flower. Only a few strands are needed for each dish.

Semolina (sooji/rava): This type of flour is available in fine, coarse, or medium grains. It is made from processed wheat with the wheat germ removed. Semolina is used to make desserts and savory porridge.

Sev: Sev are very fine fried noodles made with chickpea flour. They are eaten as is or sprinkled on snacks.

Tamarind: This is a pod of the tamarind tree. It has a sour and slightly sweet taste that helps balance the spiciness of some Indian dishes (e.g., sambar and rasam). Tamarind is sold in various forms: blocks, pods, and in jars of tamarind paste or concentrate.

Tempering (tadka): This is the seasoning process, either the first or the last step in Indian cooking. Spices or aromatics are fried in oil to add flavor to it. This in turn adds flavor to the dish.

Turmeric (haldi): Fresh turmeric is a rhizome like gingerroot. Ground turmeric has a vibrant color and a bitter taste that mellows after cooking. This is another spice where a little goes a long way.

Vermicelli (seviyan): These very fine noodles are made from wheat flour. They are used in both sweet and savory preparations.

Yellow split peas (chana dal): These yellow legumes are split and hulled. They are quite firm and tend to keep their shape even after cooking for a long time.

Yogurt: Yogurt is made fresh almost daily in households around India. It is served with nearly every meal either as a raita or just plain. Store-bought, whole-milk plain yogurt is the best to use in the recipes for the best consistency and flavor. Homemade yogurt is simple to make at home.

Index

Acknowledgments

I would like to thank God for giving me this opportunity and guiding me through this process.

To my husband, Harsha, for supporting the idea of my leaving the corporate world and for believing in me following my passion.

To my kids, Dhruva and Disha, who make me feel like the best "Mom-chef" out there.

To my dad, who is watching over me from above and helping me achieve my dreams.

To my mom, for giving me the cooking bug and for answering all my phone calls at any hour of the day.

To my sister and nieces, for amazing virtual support and for being my cheering squad.

To my cousins for being my recipe testers and providing valuable feedback.

To my NJ friends, for their unconditional love and encouragement.

To Callisto Media, for believing in me and giving me this opportunity to write my first cookbook. Special thanks to Gurvinder, for helping me deliver the best version possible.

Last but definitely not least, my sincere thanks to my family, friends, and blog readers for your continuous encouragement and support.

About the Author

 **Pavani Nandula** is an engineer who shifted gears to follow her passion for cooking. She is the cook, creator, and photographer behind the blog *Cook's Hideout*, which she founded in 2006 and which was recognized as one of the top Indian food blogs. Her recipes have been featured in BuzzFeed, Brit + Co, *Country Living*, and LiveKindly.co. She is a lifelong vegetarian who loves trying out new recipes from different cuisines for her family and friends. Her blog focuses on easy-to-make, approachable, family-friendly recipes. She likes converting traditional meat-based recipes into vegetarian or vegan dishes. When she is not working, blogging, or cooking, Pavani loves to binge-watch Netflix shows or read mystery novels. She lives in Denver, Colorado, with her husband and two kids.

For more of Pavani's work, follow her on CooksHideout.com and on social media:

Facebook: Facebook.com/cookshideout

Instagram: Instagram.com/cooks_hideout

Or send her an email: cookshideout@gmail.com

CPSIA information can be obtained
at www.ICGtesting.com
Printed in the USA
JSHW010336221021
19659JS00003B/4